Standard Paper-Ba

CW01064486

Emma Paddock Telford

Alpha Editions

This edition published in 2024

ISBN : 9789362094841

Design and Setting By
Alpha Editions
www.alphaedis.com
Email - info@alphaedis.com

As per information held with us this book is in Public Domain.
This book is a reproduction of an important historical work. Alpha Editions uses the
best technology to reproduce historical work in the same manner it was first
published to preserve its original nature. Any marks or number seen are left
intentionally to preserve its true form.

Contents

FOREWORD

In giving this little book to the public, there has been in mind one thing—practicability.

The endeavor has been to make the directions for "Paper-bag Cookery" so clear and concise that even the inexperienced housekeeper may not be deterred from trying this new-old way of cooking foods delicately, digestibly, economically.

No one is advised to try dishes—as for instance soups, omelettes, macaroni and kin,—and many desserts that may better be done by other methods.

Neither has the author called for strange and divers seasonings and materials that are only to be found in the kitchens of the mighty and their attendant chefs.

For the very large family or boarding house, pots and pans need still be called upon; but for the small family, for the woman who does her own work and wishes to minimize labor, or for the epicurean but frugal housewife who looks personally after the details of her own little establishment, this paper-bag cookery is commended. If this little volume points the easiest way for the preparation of nice dishes with a modicum of labor and a saving of time and money, it is all that its author and compiler asks.

CHAPTER I.

WHAT IS PAPER BAG COOKERY?

THE principles contained in Paper-bag Cookery are not new. Woodsmen and hunters have known for ages that if they wanted fish or game done to a turn, a jacket of clay outside the meat which was protected from soil by leaves or corn husks, gave, on removing the clay case, the very quintessence of delicate, savory cookery.

Now within the last two years, a series of experiments has resulted in the perfecting of a system of Paper-bag Cookery that revolutionizes the old time kitchen drudgery with its unending round of greasy pots and pans to be taken into account.

The advantages of this method of cooking are manifold. They may be epitomized thus:

I. It makes food more savory and nutritious.

II. It is sanitary. No dust can reach the article being cooked and, the cooking accomplished, the bag can be thrown into the stove or kitchen scrap basket with no temptation for a lazy maid to tuck away a greasy pan in the dish closet for the delectation of "germs" or roaches.

III. It is economical. Not only does it save the time and strength of the housewife with no aftermath of dirty cooking dishes to be washed, but it prevents the shrinkage of meats as caused by ordinary cookery. Nothing is lost, because there is no evaporation; careful experiments prove that the weight of the cooked food tallies almost exactly with the weight of the raw. There is also a great saving of fuel, some claiming as high as 40 per cent., owing to the less time required in Paper-bag Cookery. While this may be a generous estimate it is certain that Paper-bag Cookery takes on the average, one-third less time than other cooking.

IV. With ordinary care there is no danger of food burning, and no deterioration in flavor if left in the bag some little time before serving.

V. It is odorless; a great thing, this, for the flat-dweller who has to cook in restricted quarters, taking care always that cooking odors do not permeate the house.

VI. Its price is not prohibitive. Indeed, it is most reasonable.

Paper-bag Cookery calls for no big outlay of money, no patent stove oven, no complex apparatus or appliances. All that is necessary is an oven of any sort—coal, gas, electric, wood or oil—a broiler, a paper bag specially and sanitarily prepared,—grease proof and waterproof,—a wood cookery dish if the food contains liquid or a number of separate ingredients, and something to cook therein. Another convenience are the wire clips for fastening the mouth and corners of the bag, which can be purchased wherever the bags are sold.

THE KIND OF PAPER BAG TO USE.

While a sheet of heavy foolscap paper made into a bag serves for the cooking of a single chop—it is self-evident that for larger proportions, larger bags and bags from strong, absolutely sanitary paper must be used. While there are bags and bags now upon the market, not all fulfill these essential conditions. After much experimenting, the Continental Paper Bag Co., of Rumford, Maine, and New York City, has succeeded in producing the ideal bag which may now be found in varying sizes, at all the large house-furnishing stores, grocers, butchers, etc., or the bags may be ordered direct from headquarters. These bags are put up in bulk in bundle lots, or in sealed packages of assorted sizes. Each of the sealed packages contains thirty bags of assorted sizes with the necessary clips and a small book of recipes with full directions. Retail price 25 cents a package—fifty packages to a shipping bundle.

In order to make paper bag cookery of the greatest value to housewives, both as regards cleanliness and ease of operation, to say nothing of the many cases where the flavor of the food is actually improved, the author heartily recommends the use of specially prepared wood cookery dishes. These dishes are most inexpensive, varying in price from about thirty for ten cents to six for ten cents, depending upon size. They can be purchased wherever the paper bags are sold,—department stores, house furnishing stores, grocery stores, etc., etc., or may be obtained direct from the Oval Wood Dish Company, Delta, Ohio. The food is placed in the wood cookery dish and the dish is put into the bag. The advantage lies in the fact that should the bag break, the food and juices are saved in the dish and the oven will not be soiled by leakage. Then again, the food can be removed from the bag when finished with greater ease than when the dish is not used. The dishes are so cheap that they can be thrown away with the bag after the food is prepared.

CHAPTER II.

GENERAL DIRECTIONS FOR USING THE BAG.

I. SELECT a bag that fits the food to be cooked. When a liquid is used or a number of ingredients are to be cooked together, use a wood cookery dish which holds the food stuffs together and permits their ready removal from the bag.

II. Brush over the outside of the bag with a little water to make it pliable. Grease the inside except in the case of vegetables or when water is added, using for this another little flat brush (kept for this purpose) and pure vegetable oil, melted butter or drippings. Apply the brush with a rotary motion greasing the bottom first and working toward the top; or lay the bag flat on a table, reach inside and grease the lower side of the bag, then press the other side against it until both surfaces are evenly greased. The up-to-date housewife who is adopting the paper-bag culinary cult has also discovered that for greasing the bags, a necessary step, there is nothing that can take the place of the high grade vegetable oils. They are easily applied and absolutely tasteless and odorless, a great point, this, when the bags themselves have sometimes been condemned as imparting a foreign odor to foods cooked in them, when in reality it was the fault of the special fat with which they were greased. Now place the bag flat on the table, seam side up and lift the uppermost side while you insert the article to be cooked. Press the air out of the bag, fold over the corners and make two folds of the mouth of the bag, fastening firmly with three or four clips, or even pins. No harm is done if the two lower corners of the bag are folded and also fastened with one clip each.

III. Now be sure the oven heat is right. If you are using gas for the cooking, light for five minutes before the bag goes into the oven. The average oven heat should be not less than 200 degrees Fahrenheit, and may be 250 degrees. When the bag is put into the oven, the heat must be at once reduced to 170 degrees. An inexperienced cook lacking an oven thermometer can test the right degree of heat by placing a bit of paper in the oven and noting the color it assumes. At the end of five minutes it should be a light golden brown.

If the heat is too intense the bag will burst. Now carefully lay the bag on the grid shelves or wire broilers—never on solid shelves, being careful to *place the seam side of the bag up.*

This is imperative, as otherwise the juices of the food being cooked may cause the seam to open, and distribute its contents over the oven. Once placed in position, roasts and entrees on the lower shelf, about an inch from the oven floor, fish on the middle shelf, and pastry on the top where heat is most intense,—do not move or open the bags until the schedule time of their cooking is accomplished. In placing the article to be cooked, take care that the bag does not touch the sides of the oven and that it is not too close to the flames. When the time limit of cooking has expired, take up the bag from the shelf by drawing *with* the wires, not across them, which is apt to tear the bag made tender by charring. Slip on to the lid of a pot or flat tin held just beneath the grid and thence to the heated platter. To secure the gravy, stick a pinhole in the bottom of the bag and allow it to drain on to the platter, or serving dish. Rip open the bag from the top and throw the charred fragments away at once. If to be served hot, arrange at once on a heated platter or other dish, with its appropriate garnish.

POINTERS FOR PAPER BAG COOKERY.

I. In the case of a coal-heated oven with solid shelves a wire broiler or "grid" should be substituted as the heat must be allowed to circulate on all sides of the bag.

II. The size of the oven makes no difference but it *must be kept clean.*

III. In the case of a fowl or joint see that there are no rough edges or bones protruding that will be likely to pierce the bag.

IV. Do not season the article to be cooked too highly as none of the seasonings are dissipated during the cooking as is usually the case in ordinary boiling or roasting.

V. For cooking fruit, grease the outside of the bag.

VI. In removing the bag from the oven, draw with the wires, not across them.

VII. To brown things at the last of the cooking, if necessary, puncture a few holes in the top of the bag.

VIII. If a bag breaks in the cooking, as it sometimes will if the heat is too intense, do not try to remove the article being cooked from the bag, but slip the whole into a new well-greased bag. The use of two bags is better than one when things require long cooking or for meats with much fat or juicy dishes. While it may cost a bit more, it will save much anxiety lest the bag burst.

IX. To avoid having any chance drippings soil the oven floor, slip a thin tin baking sheet or shallow dripper under the broiler, letting it rest flat on the bottom of the oven. Put in a little hot water and this steam will keep the bag moist and do much to discourage its breaking. Indeed, in baking any kind of fruit cake, which requires slow cooking, quite a little water in the drip-pan underneath is advisable.

X. In baking pastry and cake, a few tiny holes should be made in the upper side of the bag before putting in the oven. This will brown the surface of the cake delicately.

XI. Do not let the bag touch the sides of the oven or the gas flames.

XII. Wire trivets such as are sold at house-furnishing stores for use in cooling bread and cakes will be found a great convenience. If a bag is laid on a trivet, it can then be easily set in the oven and as easily lifted out when done.

XIII. Never try to take things from the oven with the gas lighted. Matches are cheaper than gas, if the oven has to be relighted, and burned fingers or wrists are more costly than many matches.

XIV. Use care in opening the oven. A draught from an open door or window might cause the gas flame to ignite the bag.

XV. Until taught by experience, follow the time table as given in the cookery book.

CHAPTER III.

As a general rule less time is required for Paper-bag Cookery than any other way. While this approximate time table is at your service, experience will enable you to modify the figures to suit your own stove and your family's predilections as to having things rare or well done.

FISH.

1 lb.	15 minutes
3 lbs.	30 minutes
6 lbs.	50 minutes

ROASTS.

Beef, 3 lbs.	45 minutes
Add 5 minutes for each additional pound.	
Veal, 5 lbs.	1 hour and a half.
Add 7 minutes for each additional pound.	
Pork, 3 lbs.	50 minutes
Add 6 minutes for each additional pound.	
Mutton, leg 8 pounds	An hour and a half
Mutton, shoulder 5 pounds	45 minutes
Mutton, chops	12 minutes
Mutton, cutlets	8 minutes
Lamb, leg 7 lbs.	$1\frac{3}{4}$ hours.
Lamb, shoulder	50 minutes
Lamb, chops	10 minutes
Sausages	8 minutes
Sliced Bacon	6 minutes

POULTRY.

Turkey (stuffed) 15 lbs.	2½ hours
Turkey (not stuffed) 15 lbs.	2 hours
Goose (ordinary size)	2 hours
Goose (green)	1½ hours
Duck (old)	1 hour
Duck (young)	35 minutes
Guinea, 6 lbs.	1 hour and 40 minutes
Chicken (large)	1 hour and a half
Chicken (young)	45 minutes
Quail and other small birds	15 minutes
Stews (meat) medium sized	1½ or two hours
Potatoes (Baked)	35 minutes

Sweet (ten minutes less than by the other methods of cookery).

TABLE OF MEASUREMENTS.

4 teaspoonfuls of liquid	1 tablespoonful
4 tablespoonfuls of liquid	½ gill or ¼ cupful
1 tablespoonful of liquid	½ ounce
1 pint of liquid	1 pound
2 gills of liquid	1 cupful or ½ pint
1 kitchen cupful	½ pint
1 quart sifted pastry flour	1 pound
4 cupfuls sifted pastry flour	1 quart or 1 pound
2 rounded tablespoonfuls of flour	1 ounce
1 rounded tablespoonful granulated sugar	1 ounce
2 rounded tablespoonfuls of ground spice	1 ounce

1 heaping tablespoonful powdered sugar	1 ounce
3 cupfuls cornmeal	1 pound
1 cupful butter	½ pound
1 pint butter	1 pound
1 tablespoonful butter	1 ounce
Butter size of an egg	2 ounces
10 eggs	1 pound
1 solid pint chopped meat	1 pound
2 cupfuls granulated sugar	1 pound
1 pint brown sugar	7 ounces
2½ cups powdered sugar	1 pound
1 cupful stemmed raisins	6 ounces
1 cupful rice	½ pound
1 cupful stemmed raisins	6 ounces
1 cupful cleaned and dried currants	6 ounces
1 cupful grated bread crumbs	2 ounces
8 rounded tablespoonfuls of flour	1 cupful
8 rounded tablespoonfuls of sugar	1 cupful
8 rounded tablespoonfuls of butter	1 cupful
1 common tumbler	1 cupful
3 tablespoonfuls grated chocolate	1 ounce
4 gills	1 pint
2 pints	1 quart
4 quarts	1 gallon

CHAPTER IV.

APPETIZERS AND RELISHES.

APPETIZERS play a very important part now-a-days in all up-to-date establishments and even in modest homes where they are not only employed as introductory to the course dinner, but as a pleasing accessory to the afternoon tea service. They are supposed to whet the appetite for the heavier dishes that follow. In Europe one always finds them. They are considered very "smart" and as they are but little trouble to prepare in Paper bag cookery, when one has learned the trick, there is no reason why the hostess who aims to keep abreast of the times should not make frequent use of them. At very formal affairs, they are placed on the service plates after the guests are seated, but usually they are at each place when the meal is announced. Canapés (which means "toast cushions" or bouchees, small patties or "bites") with their accompanying spread of appetizing fish, cheese or potted meats, are newer than the cocktails of oyster, clam or grape-fruit that used to lead the feast.

Bouchee Cases.—These are usually made from pastry by covering tiny but deep patty pans with rich pastry, cutting narrow strips to make the rim for the cup. Put on a tin in a buttered bag and bake. When cool they will slip from the pan. They may be made the day before using if preferred.

Another way of preparing them is to cut good sized circles of bread; then with a smaller cutter, scrape out a hollow, spread with butter, put in the bag and bake ten minutes until browned. When ready to serve, fill with any mixture desired and serve hot or cold as appetizers or with the salad course.

Bonne Bouchee.—Make the pastry cases and when ready to serve fill with pate-de-foie gras, made soft with whipped cream, seasoned with salt, cayenne or paprika. Decorate each one with an olive or bit of aspic jelly.

Bouchees of Caviare, Olives and Mayonnaise.—Spread circles or dominoes of bread with a thin layer of caviare. In the center place a pitted olive, green or black, with its pit removed and the cavity filled with minced red peppers. Hold the olive in place with a few drops of mayonnaise, red or the usual yellow, and put tiny dots of the same about the border.

Bouchees of Sardines.—Pound one or two boned sardines in a mortar, together with a small quantity of cheese. Season with salt, pepper and chili vinegar, and add, if you like, a few chopped oysters. Spread this mixture on circles of "bagged" bread about the size of a silver dollar, and add a garnish of hard-boiled yoke of egg, rubbed through a sieve and a little finely minced parsley.

Bouchees of Sausage or Tongue.—Cover circles of "bagged" bread with red stars cut from boiled tongue or the red imported sausages. Lay on the top of each star, log cabin fashion, several tiny lengths of pickled gherkins and crown with a sprig of watercress.

The Making of Canapés.—Bread two days old is best for the foundation. Trim free from crusts, then cut in uniform oblongs, diamonds, triangles, circles or fingers as desired, using for this the cutters that come on purpose. Butter lightly, spread with the prepared mixture and slip into the well-greased paper-bag for five minutes just long enough to brown the toast delicately and heat the savory.

Anchovy Canapés.—Cut white bread in oblong strips, spread lightly with butter, and anchovy paste, and tuck into the buttered bag. Bake five minutes, then serve hot, adding, if liked, to each canapé two strips of boneless anchovy laid across it diagonally and a squeeze of lemon juice.

Caviare Canapés.—Cut bread in circles and spread with a mixture of three tablespoonfuls caviare paste, one teaspoonful lemon juice, one half teaspoonful paprika, two tablespoonfuls of butter, and a half cupful minced cress. Pop in the buttered bag and cook five minutes.

Hot Cheese Canapés.—Take circles or strips of Vienna bread, spread lightly with butter, grate a little cheese over them, sprinkle on top a little cayenne pepper and salt and put in bag. Cook five minutes.

Cheese and Cracker Canapés.—Split Boston crackers and soak ten minutes in cold water. Lift out carefully and place on a well-buttered baking tin. Drop on each a generous bit of butter, a sprinkling of grated Parmesan or American cheese and a dusting of paprika. Put in the bag, seal and bake fifteen minutes in a hot oven.

Cheese Toast Sandwiches.—Cut slices of white bread rather thicker than for sandwiches. Chop fine one cupful of American cheese and two green peppers with the seeds removed. Season with salt and pepper and work to a paste. Spread one slice of bread with butter and its mate with creamed filling. Press firmly together, take off the crusts, and put into the buttered bag. Bake five minutes and serve very hot.

Cracker Crisps.—Dip oyster crackers or dinner biscuits in melted butter, sprinkle with Parmesan cheese, and put in a paper bag. Bake ten minutes.

Deviled Crackers.—Mix three tablespoonfuls of grated cheese, one-fourth teaspoon of dry mustard, one teaspoon of anchovy paste, a dash of cayenne and a pinch of butter. Spread over the crackers and put in bag in a hot oven to brown.

Diables à Cheval.—Have ready large French prunes that have been soaked twenty-four hours in water, then cooked and the pits removed. Insert almonds in the cavity left by the pit. Toss in olive oil or refined cotton seed oil or roll in thin slices of bacon, fastened with a tooth pick, put in the bag, seal and cook eight minutes. Serve piping hot.

NUT APPETIZERS.

Salted Almonds.—Shell as many nice large nuts as desired. The Jordan nuts are best, but the paper-shelled ones will answer. Put into a bowl and cover with boiling water. Spread a towel over the bowl to retain the steam and let them stand five minutes. Pour off the water and replace with cold, then rub off the brown skins between thumb and forefinger. Shake in a colander until dry, then put in a shallow dish adding for each cupful of nuts, one tablespoonful melted butter, olive or refined cotton seed oil (preferably either of the oils, which will give the richer glaze). Stir well together. Let stand an hour, then put into the well-greased paper bag, first sprinkling with dry salt, allowing one tablespoonful to each cupful of nuts. Fasten and roast ten minutes, shaking the bag occasionally. You can do this by the aid of two trivets.

Deviled Almonds.—To devil them, add a suspicion of cayenne pepper with the salt.

Roasted Chestnuts.—Make a cross on the shell of the nut using a sharp penknife. Put in the oiled bag, dredge lightly with salt, and let cook twenty minutes giving an occasional shake.

Salted Chestnuts.—Throw into boiling water as many shelled nuts as desired. Blanch and dry, patting with a soft towel. Then add olive oil or melted butter to the nuts, allowing a teaspoonful to each cup of nuts and let them remain in oil half an hour. Dredge with salt, a heaping teaspoonful to each cup, then put in oiled bag and let them brown in the oven from 10 to 15 minutes, shaking the bag frequently to keep them from scorching and make them an even brown. These should be crisp and delicate. To devil them, add a suspicion of cayenne with the salt. Serve at dinner after the cheese.

Deviled Chestnuts.—Shell and blanch a quart of chestnuts. Dry thoroughly, then brown in paper bag in hot olive oil or butter. Have ready a mixture composed of two tablespoonfuls of chopped mixed pickle, one tablespoonful Worcestershire sauce, one quarter teaspoonful salt and a dash of cayenne. Turn this over the hot nuts, and serve at once.

CHAPTER V.

SOUP ACCESSORIES.

Bread Sticks.—IN preparing these, any bread dough may be used, though that with shortening is preferred. After it is kneaded enough to be elastic, cut into pieces half the size of an egg, then roll on the molding board into a stick the size of a pencil and about a foot long. Lay these strips in the well-greased paper bag, let them rise a little before putting in the oven, then fasten the bag and bake with a moderate heat, so they will dry without much browning.

Croutons Toasted.—Slice bread that is stale but not too dry, into pieces about half an inch thick, cut these slices in uniform cubes and put in a well-greased bag. Shake occasionally and let toast for ten minutes.

Crisped Crackers.—Split butter crackers and spread with butter. Put into the paper bag buttered side up and bake ten minutes. These are delicious with vegetable soups and in fish chowder and oyster stew.

Egg Balls.—Drop the yolk of four eggs into a cup and set in a pan of water over the fire. When the yolks are cooked hard and mealy, pound to a paste and season with an even teaspoonful of salt, a pinch of cayenne or a more liberal sprinkling of paprika. Mould into balls the size of grapes, by mixing the yolk of a raw egg with the cooked paste, rolling lightly in the white of an egg, then in flour. Tuck into a small buttered bag, fasten, and set in oven for five minutes to become firm.

Forcemeat Balls or Quenelles.—Chop very fine any cold meat you have on hand, and season with salt, pepper, chopped parsley and a little onion juice. For one cupful of the prepared meat, beat one egg until light, stir in with hashed meat and add just enough flour to make cohesive. Roll in the hands to the size of hickory nuts, put in paper bag and cook ten minutes.

CHAPTER VI.

SHELL FISH.

FISH and the paper bag method of cooking, go hand and glove. The thing that every housewife hates most, particularly in a small apartment, or in the Winter when it is difficult to get the house thoroughly aired, is the pervasive odor that announces to every one in the house or block just what you are going to have for dinner. Bagged, the odor is so minimized as to be entirely inoffensive. Ten minutes airing after the bag is opened will be quite sufficient to dissipate every particle of odor. Furthermore, the fish itself is much more delicate and digestible with all the flavor of fish and seasoning held in and united in a harmonious whole. Of course, this presupposes a fresh fish to start with, or one just out of cold storage, before it has had a chance to thaw and develope ptomaines. In buying fish, look at the eyes and flesh. Fish should be firm to the touch. If pressed by the finger the flesh should rise instantly. There should be no impression left. If fish is fresh the eyes are bright and the gills red and the scales not easily rubbed off. Never lay fish directly on artificial ice, say the fishermen, as the ammonia used in the freezing affects them injuriously. Shell fish are not so apt to spoil as the other fish.

The wood cookery dishes will be found of great value in cooking all kinds of fish in paper bags. In many cases the flavor of the fish is improved and the fish can always be taken from the bag with ease and served whole if desired.

Clam Pies.—Line little tins or moulds with paste and put in a layer of raw clams with a seasoning of butter and pepper. Dredge with flour, add a spoonful or two of clam juice, cover with the paste, cut a hole in the top, brush with beaten egg, slip into the bag, fasten and bake twenty minutes.

Roast Clams.—Scrub the shells clean and slip in the bag. As soon as the shells open, remove carefully and pour off the extra liquor in as many small cups as you have persons to serve. Put a cup of the juice to which a bit of butter and dusting of pepper has been added, in the center of a soup dish, and arrange the clams around it. With an oyster fork, the clams may then be removed from the shell, dipped into the liquor and eaten. Serve very hot with quarters of lemon.

Crabs, Soft and Hard.—While soft shell crabs are too expensive for the purse of moderate depth, the hard shell crustacean is always in order and greatly to be desired. Crabs, like all other shell fish, are best when fresh from their native waters, and the individual who can do his own crabbing and then eat the fruits of his labor with the flavor of the sea still with them, has nothing more to be desired from a gastronomic standpoint. In most markets crabs may be found both alive and boiled. If alive, keep them in cold water until ready to cook. If already boiled, use them as soon as possible as they do not keep well for more than twenty-four hours. When ready to cook live crabs, take up on a skimmer, handling gingerly so as to avoid a pinch, and drop into a large kettle of boiling salted water. Cook gently fifteen minutes, or until a bright red, skim out, and cool, twist off the claws, remove the upper shell from the under, scrape the spongy portions from the sides, remove the green portion and wash free from sand. Crack the large claws and remove the meat. If you are to serve the crab meat in the shells, wash and dry as many of the upper ones as desired. These preliminaries attended to, the crabs are ready to use, in any one of a dozen different ways.

Creamed Crabs.—Remove the meat from a half dozen hard-shelled crabs. Cook two tablespoonfuls of butter and a tablespoonful of finely chopped onion until yellow, add two tablespoonfuls of flour, and pour in gradually a cup of cream. As soon as blended and smooth, add the crab meat, salt and paprika to season, a tiny grating of nutmeg and a tablespoonful of sherry wine. Spread on slices of toast, grate a little cheese on top, put into a bag, seal, set in the oven a moment to heat through, then serve.

Crabs Deviled à la William Penn.—Boil hard-shelled crabs, then remove the under part without breaking the upper shell. Take out the crab meat, add about half the quantity of bread crumbs and some chopped hard boiled eggs, with salt, cayenne and lemon juice to season. Form into a paste with a little melted butter and fill the shells. Sift buttered crumbs over the top, slip in the bag and cook ten minutes in a hot oven.

Crab Meat au Gratin.—Mix the meat from six crabs with a third the amount finely chopped, sweet, green peppers. Add the yolks of two eggs beaten with a half cup cream and a little sherry, and toss in a saucepan until hot and creamy. Put the mixture into the cleaned crab shells or the little brown ramequins, sprinkle with Parmesan cheese and fine crumbs; put in bag and crisp in a hot oven.

Crab Flakes au Gratin.—Add to one pint crab flakes, one-half cupful cream sauce, two tablespoonfuls melted butter and a quarter teaspoonful paprika. Mix well together, place in a small wood cookery dish or ramequins, sprinkle the top with toast crumbs and a light sprinkling of Roman cheese. Put into bags, bake and serve. If any be left over, it makes a delicious salad served on lettuce with mayonnaise.

Lobster Chops.—Put into a saucepan a heaping tablespoonful of butter and two very heaping ones of flour. As soon as melted and frothed, add one cupful of hot milk or cream, and stir until the mixture is smooth and thick. Season with salt and paprika, take from the fire, add two cups of the lobster, cut fine, mix well and turn on to a platter to get as cold as possible. When cold and firm, form into balls, then flatten into chops, roll in egg, then in cracker crumbs and set away on the ice until ready to cook. Put in buttered paper bag and cook ten minutes. When ready to serve, tuck one of the little claws in the small end to simulate a chop bone and garnish with lemon and parsley. For Sunday night supper these chops may be cooked early in the day, then simply re-bagged and heated in the oven for the meal.

Coquilles of Lobster.—Cook two tablespoonfuls of finely chopped onion in a tablespoonful butter for fifteen minutes. Have ready a cream sauce made by melting together over the fire a tablespoonful each of butter and flour, then thinning with a cupful of white stock that has been cooked with a small bouquet of sweet herbs. Salt and pepper to taste, and if you like add half a cupful chopped mushrooms and their liquor. Add to the lightly browned onions two cupfuls finely cut lobster meat, a tablespoonful minced parsley, one cupful of the made sauce and salt and paprika. Cook together ten minutes, then put the mixture into the shells, pour a little of the sauce over each, sprinkle with buttered bread crumbs, bag, and bake about ten minutes or until they are browned.

Lobster in Shells.—Cut the meat from two cans of lobster into small pieces. Sprinkle a few bread crumbs and a little salt and pepper over it. Then put in shells. On each shell put a good sized lump of butter, two teaspoonfuls of wine, some more salt and pepper and some more bread crumbs. Put prepared shells in a paper bag, put in a hot oven and cook ten minutes.

Mussels au Gratin.—Remove and clean the mussels, straining all the liquor thoroughly. Then make this sauce: Fry two tablespoonfuls of chopped onions in butter for a few minutes, but do not let them brown; add about a teaspoonful of flour, and, while the onions are blending, add the liquor of the mussels, stirring it in slowly. Cook this mixture for a few minutes; then add a tablespoonful of vinegar, the same quantity of chopped parsley and pepper and salt to taste. Butter a shallow earthen or wooden baking dish; in the bottom spread a layer of the sauce, lay the mussels on top of it and cover them with the balance of the sauce. Over all this spread a thin coating of breadcrumbs; butter and bake in bag until they have browned. Serve in the same dish in which they were baked.

Boxed Oysters (Virginia Style).—Take crusty rolls, cut off the top and scoop out the hearts leaving them each like a box. Fill the space with oysters, seasoning with salt, pepper and butter and sprinkling over them some of the crumb of the roll that you have removed. Put bits of butter on top, then replace the cover. Set the rolls in the buttered bag and pour the strained oyster liquor over them. Put into a hot oven and bake for fifteen minutes. Serve hot. Lemon juice or a little mace is sometimes used for seasoning the oysters.

Spindled Oysters and Bacon.—For two dozen large oysters have two dozen thin slices bacon, and a half dozen slices crisp toast. Have ready a half dozen slender steel skewers. Fill these skewers with alternate slices of bacon and oysters, running the skewer crosswise through the eye of the oyster and threading the bacon by one corner, so that each slice blankets an oyster. Do not crowd. Lay the skewers in a buttered bag, and cook in a quick oven ten minutes. Lay each spindle with its contents undisturbed on a slice of toast, pour the drip from the bag over them and serve at once.

CHAPTER VII.

FISH.

Filet of Bass.—WASH and wipe the filets dry with a clean towel, trimming away the fins with a pair of large scissors close to the filet. Dust with salt and lay in a covered dish with a minced onion, the juice of half a lemon and a bit of finely cut parsley and thyme. Let them stand half an hour. Twenty minutes before serving wipe dry again, dust lightly with flour, dip in well-beaten egg, then roll in fine bread crumbs. When all are prepared, put in greased bag and cook twenty minutes until a delicate brown. Arrange on a warm dish and serve with parsley and lemon or sauce tartare. Filets of sole may be cooked in the same way.

Baked Blue Fish.—Clean thoroughly, cut off head and tail and fill with a soft bread stuffing. Tie up securely, rub over the outside of the fish with sweet vegetable oil, sprinkle with salt and pepper, add a squeeze of lemon juice and slip into the greased bag. Seal and cook from twenty to forty minutes according to weight. Serve with sliced lemon rolled in fine cut parsley.

A Breakfast Dish of Bloaters.—Few people know how very nice smoked and dried fish can be when cooked in a paper bag and seasoned in the French fashion. Cut off the head and tail of the fish, loosen the skin at the neck with a knife and holding it firmly between the knife and finger, pull it off. Split the fish with a sharp knife, remove the backbone and soak in cold water over night, or if you forget to do that, for twenty minutes in water nearly at the boiling point. Arrange the filets in a wooden baking dish, cover with milk, dot with bits of butter, put in bag and bake in a hot oven for fifteen minutes. Garnish with a little finely chopped parsley or sprigs of water cress and serve with paper-bag baked potatoes. On a cool morning there are few more appetizing breakfast dishes, while its cheapness puts it within the reach of the most impecunious. For a change the filets may be baked in buttered paper cases or cooked au gratin still in paper bags.

Cat Fish.—For the small sized cat fish—clean, wash, dry well, salt and pepper inside and out, then grease well with butter or vegetable oil and roll in fine, sifted bread crumbs or corn meal. Lay in a well-greased bag on thin sliced bacon, put a few more slices of bacon on top. Seal and cook half an hour.

Codfish Cones.—"Pick up" enough salt codfish to make two cupfuls of the shreds. Cover with cold water and let stand for two hours, then drain, make a cream sauce, using two level tablespoonfuls each butter and flour, and one cupful of hot milk. Mash and season enough hot boiled potatoes to measure two cupfuls, add sauce and fish and beat well with a fork. Shape in small cones, brush with melted butter, dredge with fine bread crumbs and put in a paper bag. Cook ten minutes. If desired some thin slices of bacon can be cooked at the same time in a separate bag and be used as a garnish for the cones.

Codfish à la Crême.—Cook the fish first in boiling salted water which has been very slightly acidulated with vinegar. Let it cook until the flesh separates from the bones. After draining thoroughly and removing the skin and bones, break the flesh into large flakes. Pour a highly seasoned white sauce over it. It may now be cooked in a wooden baking dish in the bag, or it may be prepared as follows: Press it into the form of an oblong mould, using only just enough sauce to hold the flakes together. Not as much sauce is needed as when the fish is browned in a baking dish. Brush the top liberally with melted butter, sprinkle with rolled cracker crumbs. Put the mold in a paper bag in the oven, and let the fish acquire a nutty, crisp crust. Send to the table garnished with lemon and parsley or thin slices of tomato and a few sprays of water cress.

Paper Bagged Eels.—Eels may be cooked in a paper bag without growing as hard as they are apt to do as ordinarily treated. Allow one-half pound of eels (after they are dressed) to a person. Wash them thoroughly, removing all blood from slit in eels. Cut in two-inch pieces, put in a dish and sprinkle a teaspoonful of salt to every pound over them. Now pour over them boiling water, enough to cover well, and let stand until water is cold. Pour water off and leave eels where they will drain until nearly dry. Take sufficient Indian meal to roll them in, add a little pepper to it and roll each piece until well covered. Place in a well-greased bag and cook about twenty minutes, when they will be a rich brown, thoroughly cooked and deliciously juicy.

Flounder à la Meuniére.—Chop a small shallot and mix with a teaspoonful of anchovy paste, a squeeze of lemon juice, an ounce of butter, a little chopped parsley, a dash of cayenne, salt and pepper to taste. Put the fish with the seasoning inside of a well-buttered bag, after dredging the fish with flour. Pour a tablespoonful of melted butter over the fish, seal up and cook. A two-pound fish, whole, requires thirty minutes. The same weight of filets cook in eight minutes.

Filets of Flounder.—Remove the filets from a medium sized flounder and cut each filet in two. Season with salt and pepper and a few drops of lemon juice and fold each filet in two or roll up skin side inwards. Put a small piece of butter, or a teaspoonful of vegetable oil on top of each and place carefully in the well-greased bag. Seal the mouth of the bag, and cook about ten minutes on the wire grid in a hot oven.

Remove from the bag, lift carefully on to a hot platter, garnish with water cress or parslied lemon slices and serve.

Finnan Haddie.—Pick out a fish that is thick through the centre, weighing about two pounds. Soak in cold water, after washing well, for an hour. Brush all over with melted butter, dredge with flour, put in a well-buttered bag, skin side down, dot with butter and pour over it a cup of hot milk. Seal securely and bake in a very hot oven twenty minutes. The fish may be served whole, or flaked—free from bones and skin—and served with cream sauce.

Finnan Haddie.—Prepare in the regular way, lay in wood cookery dish, skin side down, season with bits of butter, add a small cupful of warm milk, put in bag and seal. Bake twenty-five minutes and serve from the dish with cream sauce. This eliminates the washing of dishes with the strong fishy odor.

Fish Cakes.—Use for this two cupfuls cold fish freed from skin and bones and chopped fine, and the same amount of cooked, seasoned and mashed potatoes. Mix well, season with salt and pepper, add two tablespoonfuls vegetable oil or melted butter and two tablespoonfuls of milk. Whip the mixture until as "light as feathers." Shape into small, flat cakes of even size. Beat up an egg on a plate, then egg the cakes and roll deftly in the finest of sifted bread crumbs and again shape. Put in well-greased bag, seal and put in a hot oven. Cook about twenty minutes.

New England Fish Pie.—Have a pound of cod steak boned and cut in pieces. Roll each piece in slightly salted flour, and season with paprika or white pepper. Lay in the well-greased bag and put on top of the fish a layer of oysters with their juice and a squeeze of lemon juice. Sprinkle with a layer of finely rolled and buttered cracker crumbs, dot with a few bits of butter, seal the bag and bake slowly fifteen minutes. Have ready some hot mashed potato well seasoned with cream and butter. Take the grid and bag from the oven, tear off the top of the bag, spread the potato over the fish like a crust, brush over with a little milk mixed with a portion of an egg yolk and set back in oven for five minutes to brown and glaze, turning the grid with the bag twice during the cooking. Cut open the bag, put the fish balls on a hot platter, garnish and serve plain with a tomato sauce.

Fish Soufflé.—One pint of boiled halibut or other delicate fish, freed from bones and skin and mashed to a pulp. Season with one small teaspoonful of salt, a dash of pepper, and one teaspoonful of onion juice. Melt a large tablespoonful of butter in a saucepan, and cook in it for three minutes a tablespoonful of flour. Add slowly a cupful of milk and the seasoned fish pulp. Beat two eggs thoroughly and add the fish to them. Pour all into bag, seal and bake twenty minutes in a moderate oven, half an hour.

Planked Fish Bag-Cooked.—Planked fish responds beautifully to the paper-bag treatment, and there is no better way of developing the distinctive flavor of any of the delicate white-meated fish. The plank however should not be as thick as that usually required. It must be of hardwood, hickory, cherry, live oak, cedar or ash—well seasoned and sawed about a half inch in thickness, rounded and tapered at one end like an ironing board. This to accommodate the tail of the fish. If cooking small fish use the oval wood cooking dishes made of maple wood.

Make it very hot in the oven or under the gas flame, then grease well with vegetable oil, olive or the refined cotton seed, and lay on it the fish cleaned, split down the back, seasoned, oiled all over with the sweetest of vegetable oils or butter and spread out as flat as possible with the skin side next to the hot board. Slip into the greased bag and fasten tightly. If you use the gas oven for planking your fish, as most of us do, turn on both burners until the oven is very hot. Then set in the fish with a trivet under the bag the same as if you were cooking without the plank.

Bake from thirty to forty-five minutes, then serve piping hot on the plank which has been taken out of the bag, set on a big japanned tray and garnished with hot mashed potato pressed through a tube in rose fashion at regular intervals, alternating with mounds of peas or carrot dice, sprigs of watercress or parsley and thin slices of lemon rolled in fine minced parsley. Accompany with sauce tartare or parsley butter.

Halibut à la Poulette.—Take two pounds of halibut, arrange in filets, freeing from skin and bone; then cut into narrow strips. Season with salt, pepper and lemon juice; cut two onions in slices and lay on the filets, then set away for half an hour. At the end of this time have ready one-third cup melted butter or refined vegetable oil. Dip the filets in this, roll, skewer into shape and dredge with flour. Arrange in a well-buttered bag, seal and bake twenty minutes in a moderate oven. Serve with white sauce and two hard boiled eggs, sliced for a garnish.

Herring au Gratin.—Soak and filet the herring. Butter a bag and strew the bottom with the bread crumbs well-buttered, a layer of grated cheese and a little minced chives or parsley. Sprinkle with pepper and lay in the filets of herring, plain or alternately with sliced tomato. Cover with more crumbs, parsley, cheese and butter, close the bag, and bake fifteen minutes until a good brown.

Herrings With Herbs.—Take four dried herrings, bone them, fill the cavities with a little (about half a teaspoonful to each fish) finely minced shallot or chives, and parsley. Add a few fresh breadcrumbs and tiny bits of butter. If liked, a tiny grate of nutmeg may be added as well as a good dust of pepper. Put into a well-greased bag and bake in the oven for ten minutes. Dish up and serve as hot as possible. Other dried fish are excellent prepared in the same way.

Kedgeree.—Mix one cup of shredded fish with one cupful of boiled rice, tender and well drained. Put into a well-buttered wooden baking dish, while you prepare the sauce. Put into a saucepan one tablespoonful each of butter and flour and as soon as melted and "bubbly," add one cup of hot milk. Stir until smooth and thick, season with salt and pepper, take from the fire, add the yolks of two hard-boiled eggs, that have been rubbed through a sieve, pour over the rice and fish. Put the dish in a well-buttered bag and set in the oven until thoroughly hot and delicately browned.

Kippered Mackerel With Fine Herbs.—Cut salt mackerel into filets, lay them in a deep earthen dish and cover with boiling water. Leave in water half a minute. Take out, wipe dry, dust with coarse black pepper and put on top of each filet half a teaspoonful of minced parsley and chives or onion and a bit of butter the size of a small walnut. Grease a bag well, put in the filets; seal and cook for twenty minutes in a hot oven. Serve hot, with brown bread and butter.

Salmon Loaf.—Mince one can of salmon, removing all bits of bone. Add to it a cupful fine, stale bread crumbs, two beaten eggs, a half cupful milk and salt, pepper, parsley and lemon juice to season. Put in a wooden mould in a buttered bag and bake or steam for half an hour. Turn out and serve hot with a white or Hollandaise sauce.

Scalloped Salmon.—Put a layer of soft grated bread crumbs in the bottom of a wooden baking dish that has been well-buttered. Sprinkle the bread crumbs with salt, pepper and bits of butter. Cover with a layer of flaked salmon, seasoning with salt and pepper and pouring in some of the oil and liquor from the can. Over this spread another layer of the seasoned crumbs, then more salmon and so on until the dish is filled. Let the last layer be of buttered crumbs moistening slightly with a little milk. Spread a little soft butter over the surface and bake in a buttered bag for half an hour in a hot oven to a rich brown.

Salmon Soufflé.—Put two tablespoonfuls of butter in a saucepan and melt without browning. Add one tablespoonful of flour, stir until blended, then pour in one cup of warm milk. When thickened and smooth, add the yolk of one egg, one cup of salmon flaked, a tablespoonful of cream and a tiny bit of essence of anchovy and pepper to season. Mix carefully and well, fold in the white of one egg beaten until stiff and dry; then fill ramekins or wooden dish three-quarters full. Put in a bag and brown in a quick oven. Serve very hot. Chopped parsley may be added if desired.

Baked Shad.—In dressing the fish, cut as small an opening as possible. Wash well, dry and fill with a dressing made in this way. Pour over one cupful dry bread crumbs enough cold water or milk to moisten. Add a teaspoonful melted butter, and a teaspoonful minced parsley. Mix thoroughly and fill the fish, sewing or skewering the opening together. Use a wood cookery dish and put into a buttered bag two or three slices of wafer-thin salt pork and having salted and peppered the outside of the fish lay carefully on top the sliced pork. Lay as many more thin slices on top of the fish, or wipe over with olive oil. Seal, set in the oven and bake three-quarters of an hour in a moderate oven. Serve with sauce tartare or a good brown sauce enriched with a small glass of Madeira.

Shad Roe.—As soon as the fish comes from the water or market, plunge the roe into boiling salted water to which a tablespoonful of lemon juice or vinegar has been added. Cook gently about ten minutes, lift out with a skimmer and slip into a bowl of ice water to become firm. When ready to cook, split lengthwise if plump and full, brush over with olive oil, melted butter or refined cotton seed oil, and tuck at once into the well-greased bag. Some cooks prefer to dust the roe with fine bread crumbs, lay into beaten egg, then dust once more with sifted crumbs before "bagging". Serve simply with lemon and cress, with sauce tartare or mayonnaise, or with a sauce prepared as follows: Put into a saucepan two tablespoonfuls butter or olive oil, one tablespoonful lemon juice, and chopped parsley, and a teaspoonful Worcestershire sauce. Heat to the boiling point and pour over the roe.

Smelts.—Smelts skewered in rings, using a wooden toothpick to hold heads and tails together, dipped in milk, well floured and fried in deep fat, make an attractive fish course. The use of a wood cookery dish here is strongly recommended. The skewer can be removed before serving, as the fish will usually keep its shape. Garnish the plate on which the fish are served with cress and slices of lemon rolled in finely minced parsley. If the smelts are to furnish the main part of the meal, pile them in the center of a hot platter and surround with a border of mashed potato, or mound the potato and circle with the fish for a border.

Bagged Weak Fish.—Well grease a bag, with butter or vegetable oil. Prepare a weak fish as for frying by seasoning with salt, pepper and dredging well with flour. Rub melted butter on both sides, place it in the bag, skin side down, lightly dredge the upper side again with flour and dot with butter. Peel and cut an onion in half, put in the bag but not on the fish. Close the bag, seal and cook on the wire rack or broiler in a hot oven for twenty-five minutes.

White Fish Planked.—Remove the head and tail and bone of the fish. Wash carefully and place in wooden cookery dish, skin side down. Season with salt, pepper, bits of butter and chopped onion. Roll a half dozen oysters in cracker crumbs, place on top of fish, and put the dish in the bag. Bake forty minutes. Set the wooden dish on a hot platter and serve. The skin of the fish and remnants can be left in the dish which can then be thrown away. Halibut and mackerel are especially fine when prepared in these wood cookery dishes as it holds them intact in process of cooking and serving.

CHAPTER VIII.

FISH SAUCE.

Anchovy Sauce.—POUND three anchovies smooth with three spoonfuls of butter, add two teaspoonfuls of vinegar and a quarter of a cupful of water. Bring to the boil and thicken with a tablespoonful of flour rubbed smooth in a little cold water. Strain through a sieve and serve hot.

Quick Bearnaise Sauce.—Beat the yolks of four eggs with four tablespoonfuls of oil and four of water. Add a cupful of boiling water and cook slowly until thick and smooth. Take from the fire and add minced onion, capers, olives, pickles and parsley and a little tarragon vinegar.

Bearnaise Sauce.—This calls for four small, chopped shallots, one branch of chopped tarragon, two tablespoonfuls of wine vinegar, two raw egg yolks, two and a half ounces of hot melted butter, half a teaspoonful of chopped parsley and a teaspoonful of pepper. Put the shallots, vinegar, tarragon and pepper in a saucepan and let it stand on a slow fire until its contents are reduced to one-half their original quantity. Squeeze the mixture through a cloth into another saucepan. Add the egg yolks and beat the mixture four minutes without allowing it to boil. Then add the melted butter very gradually, still keeping the pan where there is no danger of boiling. Season with a saltspoonful of salt and a half saltspoonful of cayenne pepper. It is well to make the last an extremely scanty portion, as more may be added if desired, but none can be removed. Stir all again quite thoroughly for a minute. Add the parsley and serve.

Brown Sauce.—Brown two tablespoonfuls of flour in butter. Add two cupfuls of milk or cream and cook until thick, stirring constantly.

Curry Sauce.—Fry a tablespoonful of chopped onion in butter and add a tablespoonful of flour, mixed with a teaspoonful of curry powder. Mix thoroughly, add one cupful of cold water, and cook until thick, stirring constantly. Take from the fire, season with salt and onion juice and serve hot.

Egg Sauce.—Mix a half cup of butter, a tablespoonful of flour, and a cupful of boiling water and set the sauce pan on the stove. Stir until thickened, seasoning with salt and pepper. Add two hard boiled eggs, chopped fine, and serve.

Sauce Hollandaise.—This is really a warm mayonnaise, using butter instead of vegetable oil. It is the best sauce for serving with salmon or other boiled fish if you desire it hot. It requires a quarter pound butter, half a lemon, the yolks of two eggs, a little salt and a half teaspoonful white pepper. The secret of its successful making is to preserve an even temperature. The sauce should not approach the boiling point, as the eggs would cook and the sauce curdle. Put the eggs in a small saucepan and add the butter, gradually stirring constantly with a wooden spoon. It will soon thicken like a mayonnaise. When the butter is all in, add salt and pepper and lastly the lemon juice, stirring until well mixed. If the sauce becomes thick, add a little stock or hot water. Surround the fish with parsley and slices of lemon and serve the sauce in a bowl. A few sliced cucumbers should be served with fish.

Egg Sauce Made From the Hollandaise.—Egg sauce may be made from the Hollandaise by sprinkling with two finely chopped hard boiled eggs and a teaspoonful of parsley.

Lobster Sauce.—This is delicious with any white fleshed fish. Its foundation is Hollandaise sauce, which is also the foundation of most of the fish sauces. To make it, stir together one tablespoonful of butter, a few drops of onion juice, a bit of bay leaf (not too much), pepper to season, and the juice of a half lemon. Add a half cup of white stock or hot water and set the bowl containing the mixture in a pan of hot water and stir until the butter melts. As soon as very hot, take from the fire and stir a little of the mixture in the well-beaten yolks of one and one-half eggs, then add the rest of the sauce and return to the fire. Stir constantly for five minutes or until thickened. Add a teaspoonful of butter, half the pounded coral of a lobster and a tablespoonful of chopped lobster meat.

Maitre d'Hotel Butter.—This is perhaps the simplest and best sauce to serve on fried or broiled fish. To make it, beat a heaping tablespoonful of butter to a cream in a warm bowl; add the juice of a lemon, a half teaspoonful of salt and two teaspoonfuls of minced parsley. A grating of nutmeg or bit of chives is sometimes added. If placed on the ice this can be kept on hand a week or more. It is also excellent spread over a juicy steak.

Sauce for Broiled Shad à la Murray.—Fry the milts, and while hot mash with butter, a tablespoonful minced parsley and a teaspoonful of lemon juice. Season lightly with salt and pepper and spread over the fish when removed from the bag. Set in the oven one moment, then serve.

Parsley Butter.—To make this delectable fish sauce, mix one ounce fresh butter with a teaspoonful each chopped parsley and lemon juice, half teaspoonful chopped mixed tarragon and cress or chervil and salt and pepper to season. Spread on a plate, set on the ice until cold then shape into pats. This is nice with any fish.

Sauce Tartare.—This is one of the standbys that no housekeeper liable to the unexpected appearance of guests should be without. It can be used in an emergency for so many different things. It is delicious with fish, cold or hot, broiled or deviled chicken, tongue, beef, cauliflower or potato salad. It is easy to make, the only essentials being good materials, everything cold, and the oil added very slowly at first. After that it may be poured in in larger quantities and more frequently. Mix in a small bowl one half teaspoonful dry mustard, the same amount each powdered sugar and salt, and a quarter teaspoonful cayenne. Add the yolks of two fresh eggs, and stir. Measure out a cupful of olive oil and add a few drops at a time, stirring until it thickens. If it begins to thicken too much to stir easily, thin with a little lemon juice, adding oil and lemon alternately until you have used all the oil and two tablespoonfuls of lemon juice. Lastly beat in two tablespoonfuls of tarragon or other vinegar. This gives the regular mayonnaise, which should be smooth and thick. Now to make it into sauce tartare, add one teaspoonful finely chopped onion or onion juice, a tablespoonful of chopped pickle, capers, olives and parsley, in any proportion desired. You may use simply the sour cucumber pickle or part pickle and olives, capers, etc. This may be kept for a number of days in cold weather by keeping in glass and in a cool place.

CHAPTER IX.

POULTRY AND GAME.

Capon.—CAPON is the best of all poultry, having been specially treated and fattened for the table. They can be distinguished in the market by the head, tail and wing feathers being left intact. They are always high in price and considered great luxuries. They are cooked the same as chicken. If to be stuffed, choose a delicate dressing like oysters or chestnuts. Cut the neck off short and remove the oil bag from the root of the tail. Singe carefully, pluck out every lingering pin feather, wash quickly with a rough, clean cloth and warm—not hot—water; dash cold water over it, let drain, then wipe carefully with a soft, damp cloth inside and out. Salt lightly inside and dust with pepper, stuff with whatever dressing you elect to have, truss, fasten thin slices of bacon or salt pork over the breast and thighs, grease the entire body liberally with soft butter or vegetable oils, put into a loose fitting well-greased bag, breast down, seal, lay on a trivet, set on broiler in hot oven, let cook till bag corners turn very brown, then slack heat one-half, or even a little more if the heat is fierce, and cook from an hour and a half to an hour and three-quarters. The capon should be a golden brown all over, except on the back where it touches the bag and underneath the bacon slices. But it will be as well done everywhere as in the brown part. Cook the liver, gizzard and neck in a small separate bag, wrapping each in a slice of bacon and seasoning them with salt and pepper. Add a very little water, seal and put on to cook less than an hour before dinner time. The slow heat will make them very tender. Cooked with capon, they would be overdone. Serve with sweet potatoes Southern style, or baked apples slightly sweetened.

Chicken with Parsnips.—Wash, parboil and scrape a quart of tender parsnips. Split a Spring chicken down the back and lay in a buttered bag, skin side up. Arrange the sliced parsnips around the chicken, sprinkle with salt and pepper, dot with bits of butter until a half cup has been used, and top with two or three thin slices of fat, salt pork. Put a half cup hot water in the bag and bake to a delicate brown. Put the chicken on a hot platter and arrange the parsnips around it. Make a cream gravy from the drippings in the bag and serve with mashed potatoes, currant jelly and beet greens.

Chicken à la Baltimore.—Take two small Spring chickens, prepare as for broiling, but cut into joints. Wipe dry, season well with salt and pepper, dip into beaten egg, then cover well with bread crumbs. Place in a well-buttered bag, pour a little melted butter or oil over them and bake in the oven twenty or twenty-five minutes. Serve with cream sauce and garnish with thin, crisped slices of bacon and tiny corn oysters.

Chicken Croquettes.—This may be made from left-over cooked chicken or from canned chicken. For a dozen croquettes allow one cupful of solid meat chopped fine, a cupful of cream sauce, made by cooking together four tablespoonfuls of butter and two of flour, then stirring in a scant cupful of hot milk and cooking until smooth and thick. Combine chicken and sauce, season with half a teaspoonful each plain and celery salt, a teaspoonful of onion juice, a little lemon juice and chopped parsley. Mix thoroughly, then set the mixture away to cool. When cool and stiff roll in finely powdered bread crumbs so that every bit of the chicken is covered and shape into cones, cutlets or cylinders. Have ready a beaten egg to which a scant tablespoonful of milk has been added, dip the croquettes in this, drain well, roll in crumbs again, and again set aside to cool and stiffen. When ready to cook, slip in well-buttered bag and bake in a hot oven twenty minutes.

Paper Bagged Chicken.—Split the chicken down the middle of the back, spread flat, and put a skewer in each side to prevent it from curling. Beat up a very fresh egg, with a pinch of salt, black pepper to taste, an ounce of melted butter, a teaspoonful of Worcestershire sauce or something similar and a teaspoonful of made mustard. Mix well. With a brush glaze the chicken with the mixture. Place in a greased bag with bread crumbs around and over it. Be careful that the skewers do not tear the bag. Seal up tight and cook from thirty-five to forty minutes in a very hot oven.

Chicken Pie.—Disjoint two chickens and cook until tender in just enough water to cover. Remove all the thick skin and the largest bones. Line a baking dish with good paste, pack the chicken in layers and dust each with salt, pepper and flour. Pour in enough of the chicken liquor to come nearly to the top; lay on a tablespoon of butter and cover with a crust after cutting out a piece as large as the top of a small cup. Moisten the edges and press together, then ornament the top with leaves cut from the trimmings of paste. Bag and bake in a quick oven.

Paste for Chicken Pie.—Sift five level teaspoons of baking powder and one level teaspoon of salt with four cups of flour and rub in one cup of butter until like coarse meal. Mix with nearly two cups of milk or enough to make a dough that can be rolled out. This makes a more hygienic crust than where no baking powder is used.

Chicken Rissoles.—Chop fine two cupfuls chicken and dressing or any scraps left. Add two spoonfuls mashed potato, the beaten yolk of one egg, salt and pepper to season. Roll in balls, dip in beaten egg yolk, then in fine bread crumbs and place in paper bag. Bake twenty minutes.

Roast Chicken.—Cover the breast of the fowl or chicken with butter, drippings, or any refined vegetable oil or tie a piece of fat bacon over it. Place in a bag and set on broiler in a hot oven. Allow twenty-five minutes for a small Spring chicken, thirty-five minutes for a large fowl, forty-five to fifty minutes (according to size) for stuffed poultry in a moderate oven.

Saute of Chicken With Mushrooms.—Cut a young, tender chicken into joints, trim off all projecting bones, season with salt and pepper—not too highly—and brush over with melted butter. Put into a well-buttered wooden cook dish, with eight or twelve small mushrooms, cut in slices. Add a pinch of herbs, a very small onion, and a half gill of good white stock. Seal bag tight, give ten minutes in a very hot oven, then thirty in moderate heat. Take up on a hot dish and keep hot, while you make the gravy. Take for the gravy the hot liquor from the bag, put it in a bowl with the yolk of an egg beaten up in half a gill of cream. Stir hard over hot water, but do not let boil. When thoroughly blended, pour over the chicken, garnish with chopped parsley, a few mushroom heads and half moons of crisp puff paste. Serve as hot as possible.

Smothered Chicken.—Have a good sized broiler cut into joints, taking care not to leave sharp bones projecting. Salt and pepper them lightly, dredge with flour and lay in a well-greased bag upon thin slices of bacon. Cover the chicken with more bacon slices, taking care to keep the chicken spread rather flat. Add a tablespoonful of water or a couple of peeled and sliced tomatoes. Shreds of green pepper add somewhat of flavor to the tomatoes. Seal in a bag and cook for forty minutes, slacking the heat almost half after the first five minutes. Serve on a hot dish with gravy from the bag.

Ducks With Banana Dressing.—Wash with cold salt water inside and out, drain, wipe dry and season lightly with salt and pepper. Make a dressing of toasted bread crumbs mixed with an equal quantity of banana. Cut in small pieces, well seasoned with chopped celery, salt and pepper. Stuff, truss, grease all over and tie slices of bacon over the breast. Put in a well-greased bag, add the juice of a lemon, and a wine glass of sherry. Seal and put in a very hot oven. At the end of fifteen minutes reduce heat one-half and cook for fifty minutes longer.

Canvas Backs.—Draw the ducks as soon as they are received, pluck, singe and wipe them with a damp cloth, but under no conditions wash them. When ready to cook, truss, dust lightly with pepper, and salt and spread them thickly with butter or vegetable oil. A very slight dusting of flour should be given when they are put into the oven. After eighteen minutes of intense heat they are ready to serve, accompanied by toasted hominy and black currant jelly.

Chicken, Italian Style.—Chop fine one onion, one small carrot, a stick of celery and a sprig of parsley. Place in the bottom of one of the wooden cookery dishes and season with salt, pepper and two tablespoonfuls of olive oil. Lay a good sized broiling chicken cut into joints on top of the vegetables, and around the chicken a half dozen dried mushrooms that have been soaked for fifteen minutes in cold water. Put in paper bag, seal and bake forty-five minutes. Remove chicken to hot platter, add a little tomato sauce to the vegetables and stock remaining in the dish, pour over the chicken and serve.

Roast Wild Duck.—If these come from salt marshes, and have therefore a fishy taste, pick, dress, scald a moment in boiling salt water, then put in very cold water for half an hour. Drain, wipe dry and having cut a lemon in half rub all over inside and out with the juice and pulp. Then grease the outside of the duck with vegetable oil or butter, salt very lightly and put in greased bag. Seal and roast in a moderate oven for an hour. Serve with paper bag baked potatoes, tart jelly and pickles.

Roast Wild Duck No. 2.—Clean and singe your duck; have a dish with boiling water enough to cover same, in which you put a tablespoonful of salt and a little carrot; parboil for only five minutes; then take out and dry. Have apples peeled and cut in quarters; stuff the duck with them. Slice bacon and wrap about four slices around it, tied with a string, lay in a buttered bag with a teacupful of water and a little salt and pepper and roast in a very hot oven for an hour. Make a gravy from the drippings in bag thickened slightly and seasoned with lemon juice, a little curry powder and any good sauce.

Roast Wild Duck, Ohio Style.—Dress the duck as usual, then stuff with one quart of sauer kraut mixed with one sweet apple sliced and a few mixed spices to season. Place two stalks of celery in one of the wooden cookery dishes, lay the duck on top, place in bag. Seal and bake in a moderate oven for an hour and a half.

Frogs' Legs.—Scald the legs in boiling hot water for a minute or two, drain and wipe them dry, sprinkle with salt and pepper, dip in beaten egg, roll in cracker crumbs and put in a well-greased bag. The use of a wood cookery dish is recommended. Bake fifteen minutes in a hot oven. Serve hot with points of toast and slices of lemon placed around the platter.

Paper Bag Roast Goose.—For roasting, a goose should preferably be scarcely passed the gosling period, not more than a year old at the most. Its wings should be supple and tender at the pinions, its breast bone soft and pliable. Its feet smooth and yellow, and its fat white and soft. Before drawing, singe the bird, then give it a thorough bath with soapsuds and a soft scrubbing brush. The skin is so oily that cold water would make no impression, and the skin is bound to be full of dust. When purification is complete, rinse thoroughly in clear cold water, then dry and draw. Wash the inside quickly with clear water to which a little baking soda has been added, then rinse and wipe. The Germans are partial to a stuffing made of equal parts of bread crumbs, chopped apples, seeded raisins and boiled onions well seasoned with salt, pepper and butter. Americans as a rule give the preference to a potato stuffing made of mashed potato highly seasoned with onion, salt, pepper and a little butter and sage. The yolks of two eggs allowed to each pint of potato makes the dressing richer. Before trussing the goose, remove all the extra fat. This should be saved and tried out later for that sovereign remedy for croup,—"goose grease." It is of no value, however, in cooking and if left in the bird, gives a coarse, rank flavor. Season the goose on the inside with salt and pepper, then stuff and truss it into shape like a turkey. Rub over lightly with vegetable oil or butter, or cover the breast with several thin slices of fat salt pork. This keeps the skin moist. Put into a well-greased bag of goodly proportions, or better still, two bags, add a tablespoonful of cold water, seal and set in a very hot oven for fifteen minutes. Then reduce the heat about half and cook until done, allowing twenty-two minutes to the pound. Serve with apples baked in a bag, mashed turnips or squash and hot corn bread that can also be cooked in a bag.

Sage and Potato Stuffing.—Should you give the preference to the old-fashioned potato-and-sage stuffing, such as your grandmother used to make, fashion it in this way: peel and boil for half an hour a half dozen good-sized potatoes. Mash well and season with one tablespoonful salt, and a teaspoonful pepper, two tablespoonfuls of white onions minced fine, and cooked in a tablespoonful of butter and a teaspoonful of sage. Mix lightly and stuff.

Bag Roasted Young Guinea Fowl.—It is but a few years ago comparatively that the excellence of the guinea fowl for the table was duly recognized. Most people were afraid to try them. Now the guinea is not only being served in all the best restaurants, but in many private homes as well. While the young guineas make the choicest eating, the old birds are not to be despised. In stuffing the guinea any approved turkey stuffing may be used, the accompaniments being as with turkey, giblet gravy and cranberry sauce. In roasting a very little water goes into the bag, instead thin pieces of fat, salt pork are skewered across the breast and around the drum sticks.

Bag Broiled Young Guinea Hen.—For bag broiling, split down the back and flatten. Brush over with vegetable oil or melted butter, put in buttered bag and bake in gas oven or hot coal oven. Lay on a hot platter, season with salt and pepper, spread with a rounding tablespoonful butter stirred with a tablespoonful finely minced parsley, garnish with watercress and little moulds or spoonfuls of cranberry jelly and serve.

Quail.—As for cooking quail there is no better way than to roast them plain, with plenty of red pepper and a little salt. For those who prefer, an excellent way is to serve them with bacon, which supplies the fat which all game birds lack.

Take a half dozen quail, wipe with a damp cloth, split them and break the leg bones. Mix together a teaspoonful of pure olive or cotton seed oil, a dash of cayenne and a tiny bit of salt. Brush the birds with this mixture and put in well-greased bag, seal, put in oven and roast fifteen minutes. Arrange six slices of delicately browned toast on a hot platter, place the birds on the slices and baste with a mixture of good butter, minced parsley and the juice of a half dozen lemons. Garnish with slices of crisped bacon and watercress.

Quail No. 2.—Place four quail in a wooden dish with a link of sausage between the birds and a strip of bacon laid on each. Put in bag, seal, and bake twenty-five minutes.

Stuffed Quail.—Put into each bird a half prune or fat raisin, with a bit of butter and a few well seasoned bread crumbs. Wrap each bird in a slice of bacon, fastening with string or tooth picks and put in well-buttered bag. Seal and place on broiler and bake about twenty-five minutes, reducing the heat during the last half of the time.

Rabbit Cookery.—In selecting a rabbit the principal thing is to find out the age and also how long hung. A rabbit should be ripe but not gamy. Unless in cold storage, they should not be kept for more than two or three days. The age of a rabbit may be determined by testing the paw. If there is a little nut there and the paw may be broken readily between the thumb and finger the rabbit is young. If the nut has disappeared and the paw resists pressure, the rabbit is too venerable for anything but a stew. In dressing a rabbit there is a little secret that enables the cook to dispose of the gamy odor that so many object to. If the thin, muscular membrane that extends from the flank over the intestines is carefully removed before cooking, the strong flavor will go with it, leaving the flesh delightfully sweet. The gall bladder in the liver must also be removed with extreme care, so as not to break it.

Barbecued Rabbit.—Open plump young rabbits all the way down the under side, wash and clean thoroughly. Lay out flat in a pan of salt and water for an hour, with a weighted plate or saucer on top to hold under the water. Wipe dry and gash across the backbone in eight or ten places and having brushed it over with olive oil or melted butter, bag and bake in a hot oven forty-five minutes.

Lay on a hot dish, season with salt, pepper and plenty of melted butter, then set in the oven for the butter to soak in. Heat in a small cup two tablespoonfuls vinegar with one of made mustard and brush over the rabbit while boiling hot. Garnish with parsley and watercress and serve alone or with a currant jelly sauce.

Roast Rabbit.—Stuff, truss, dredge with flour and rub all over with vegetable oil, soft butter or good drippings. Season lightly with salt and paprika or black pepper, place in wood cookery dish in well-greased bag, seal and place in hot oven. Allow fifty minutes, reducing the heat at the end of the first twenty minutes.

Roast Rabbit No. 2.—For an older rabbit, put into a stew kettle whole without dividing the pieces from the body. Pour in one quart of water, add a little pinch of soda when it starts to boil, and stew gently until tender. When tender take from the broth. Meantime mix together three large cupfuls dried bread crumbs, butter the size of a walnut and salt, pepper and sage to taste. Pour enough of the broth over this to mix rather soft. Stuff the rabbit, spread with butter, sprinkle with salt and pepper, lay in a buttered bag and bake to a rich brown in a moderate oven. It will not take more than a few moments. Make a good brown gravy, adding onion browned in butter if desired. A little onion may also be added to the dressing, according to preference.

Stewed Rabbit.—Cut in eight pieces, salt and pepper and put in buttered wooden dish, set in a buttered bag with a finely chopped onion, a bunch of sweet herbs, a quarter cupful stock or hot water and a tablespoonful of flour stirred smooth with a little cold water, then blended with the hot. Seal the bag and bake forty-five minutes in a hot oven.

Reed Birds.—Most of the reed birds obtained in our markets are in reality nothing but sparrows, and those undrawn. If fed on grain, as they are in Chicago, they are really very nice. To bake, wrap each one in a thin slice of bacon or salt pork, put in buttered bag, seal and cook in a quick oven. Still more delectable are they cooked en surprise. For a half dozen covers, prepare the same number of birds, six large oval potatoes, six oysters, and some thin slices of bacon. Prepare the birds as for roasting, and tuck into each little interior an oyster, seasoned with salt and pepper. Then wrap each bird in a slice of bacon. Now, having the potatoes well scrubbed, cut off one end, and using a vegetable scoop, cut out a hollow in each large enough to hold a bird. Insert the bird, replace the end of the potato, cut off, tie in place, put in buttered bag and bake in a moderate oven. Serve as soon as done, removing the string. The flavor of the bird, oysters and potato makes a delicious combination that cannot be surpassed. Serve simply with butter, or if preferred, a mushroom or oyster sauce.

Squab.—In cleaning a squab, take care not to break the little sack that holds the entrails. Split the birds down the back, rub with salt, pepper and butter or oil. Sprinkle with cracker dust and put into well-buttered bag. Bake fifteen minutes and serve on slices of crisp, hot, buttered toast with or without a thin, crispy slice of bacon. Garnish with cress or parsley.

Barbecued Squirrel, (Southern Style.)—Get two fat squirrels, skin and draw. Cut the thin skin on each side of the stomach close to the ribs, then wipe with damp cloth. Sprinkle with black pepper but use no salt. Put a layer of fat bacon in a wooden dish, set in a well-greased bag and lay the squirrels on this bed. Cover with more thin slices of bacon pour in the bag a half cupful good broth, seal, and bake an hour in a moderate oven. Serve with grape jelly or spiced grapes.

Turkey à la Bonham.—Pick out a young hen turkey, plump and delicate with small bones. Carefully remove all pin feathers and complete the drawing which may have been imperfectly done by the butcher. Cut off the neck close to the body which will make the turkey fit in the bag better, and make a proper appearance when placed on the table. Wash thoroughly inside and out and wipe dry. For the stuffing make two kinds—one for the body and one for the breast. It is a good plan to make these different so as to suit all tastes. For the body, make a chestnut stuffing. Boil and peel one quart of large chestnuts and mash with a fork. Season with pepper, salt and a little butter. For the breast, take a pint of bread crumbs free from crusts. Fry a half onion cut fine in a very little butter or vegetable oil until tender but not brown. Season nicely with chopped parsley and thyme, not too much. Salt and pepper and moisten with one beaten egg. Fill the breast and sew body and breast neatly, pulling the skin of the breast over the stuffing, and fastening in place with the wings which should be turned back to hold the skin in place. Rub the outside of the bird with flour mixed with salt and pepper, cover the breast with slices of fat salt pork tied on. Now slip breast down into a thoroughly greased bag or preferably two bags, one outside the other, the outside one also well-greased. Lay some of the fat from the turkey or a few strips of bacon over the bag, and put on the grate, seam up. Slip under the grid on the bottom of the oven a dripping pan half full of water to keep the bird moist, and prevent any fat leaking through in case the bag should burst. Be careful not to let the bag touch the side of the oven. Light both burners of the gas stove for five minutes to get the oven hot for the start. Turn out one and roast about an hour and three-quarters for a twelve pound bird. Lift out carefully, sliding the pancake turner under it to get it out easily and put it on hot platter.

For the gravy, clean the giblets thoroughly and put to cook with the neck in water to cover well. Add one onion cut up and cook until tender. Chop fine and thicken slightly with browned flour or caramel which is simply sugar browned in a pan with a little boiling water.

Venison.—For roasting, the saddle is best. As the meat is naturally dry, it must be well larded with strips of firm fat pork. Sprinkle with salt and pepper and rub over with pork drippings. Put in large well-greased bag, add two glasses of port or claret, seal and bake in moderate oven. For a roast of three pounds, allow an hour and ten minutes. For an eight pound roast, two hours and a half. Serve very hot with red or black currant jelly.

Venison Steak.—Prepare in the regular way, place in wooden cookery dish and season with salt and pepper. Put in bag. Seal and cook an hour and twenty minutes. The wooden dishes add to the flavor of all game.

CHAPTER X.

BEEF.

Bullock's Heart.—THIS is an inexpensive portion of the beef, but a very tasty one when properly cooked. It should always be served on very hot dishes, both plates and platter. If you elect to roast your heart, put in a basin of warm water and let soak for an hour to draw out the blood. Wipe dry, brush with oil or butter and tie or skewer in shape. Put in well-greased bag and roast about two hours. Serve with a border of carrots sliced and fried.

Stewed Bullock's Heart.—Soak in a basin of warm water for an hour, then drain and wipe dry. Cut in halves, rub each side with flour and put in a frying pan with a little hot butter. As soon as browned, transfer to a buttered bag, adding four or five onions sliced and browned lightly in the same butter, together with a sprig of thyme and salt and pepper to season. Add a half cupful of water and cook slowly about three hours.

Filet of Beef.—Cut from the end of a tenderloin of beef, slices about 5/8 of an inch thick. Flatten down to about 3/8 of an inch and trim round. Salt lightly on both sides, dust with pepper, and lay in a little hot melted butter, flavored with a tiny scraping of garlic for an hour, turning three or four times in the meantime. Take out, put in a well-buttered bag, seal and cook twenty-five minutes. Serve on small pieces of toast that have been spread with butter and browned in a bag, pouring over them the juice of the meat that will have collected in the bag.

Hamburg Steak.—Hamburg steak, which is too often a delusion and a snare as furnished by the inexperienced cook, can be so manipulated in paper bag cookery as to emerge a very delectable and decorative dish. In the first place never telephone for hamburg steak nor buy that already chopped and mounded ostentatiously on a platter with a garnish of parsley. Naturally the butcher works up his trimmings and inferior cuts into this comparatively inexpensive and much patronized form. Having purchased your cut of round steak in the slice, its lack of natural fat must be made up by the addition of a little beef suet (preferably from the kidney). A piece of suet the size of a butter nut may be allowed to each pound of lean meat. Next, if possible, get the butcher to chop it by hand rather than by the easier-to-him method of running it through the meat grinder. Now having your good meat at home it may be prepared in any one of a half dozen ways. For the Hamburg steaks, press lightly together into cakes about the size of a chop. If onion is desired a little onion juice may be added with discretion, but for most tastes boiled onions served separately, to accompany the steak, will be found preferable, or a few rings of raw onion added to a lettuce salad. The closely packed Hamburg steak is bound to be tough and dry. Better add a beaten egg to hold the chopped meat together than press the small and delicate particles of meat compactly.

Season lightly, brush over with oil or melted butter and lay in buttered bag. Seal and roast for half an hour. Take up on a hot platter, season, add a little melted butter mixed with finely chopped parsley and serve hot with baked or mashed potatoes. A tomato sauce may go with the steaks or a brown gravy made from beef stock. A pleasant change in the appearance of Hamburg steak can be effected by shaping it to look like lamb chops. When these are bag broiled with a bit of macaroni in each end to simulate the chop bone they can be arranged to stand on a bed of parsley stacked against a pretty bowl containing tomato sauce or stewed tomato, a spoonful of which is to be served with each portion. The bed on which the chops are to rest may be mashed potato or peas, if preferred to the parsley.

Pot Roast.—While this does not eliminate washing the pot, the juices and flavor of the beef are so conserved that instead of the usual dry pot-roast it is moist and tender and so well worth the trouble.

Peel and slice a good sized onion and brown in a round bottomed iron pot with a piece of beef suet. Wash a four or five pound piece of bottom round, place in the pot without any water and brown quickly on all sides, turning it without piercing with a fork. When very brown add a small cup of water, push it back and let simmer for one hour, turning frequently. Season and cook for ten minutes longer, then place it in a well-greased bag, seal and put in a hot oven on a broiler, adding about a cupful of the liquid in which it was cooking, before sealing. Reduce the heat of the oven after ten minutes and cook an hour and a half to two hours according to size. Potatoes may be peeled and browned in the gravy left in the pot. When done, the liquid in the bag should be added to that in the pot and thickened for gravy, first skimming off the fat if too rich.

Rib Roast of Beef.—Grease the roast lightly with drippings or vegetable oil, season with pepper, but not with salt, dust lightly with flour and place in well-greased bag, seal, and place in a hot oven, at the end of fifteen minutes, reduce the heat one-half and continue cooking for half an hour longer in case of a three pound roast or for a seven pound one, a little over an hour.

Roast Round of Beef in Paper Bag.—Get three or four pounds of beef from top round, asking the butcher for a high chunky piece—not a slab—from the tenderest, juiciest part. Have him tie it up securely and add a piece of suet. Well grease the bag inside. Season and flour the meat, place a small piece of suet on top, insert in bag, fasten with paper clips, and put on a broiler in a hot oven, reducing the heat after about five minutes. Allow fifteen minutes for each pound. It will be a rich brown on the outside but rare and juicy. With an exceptionally sharp carving knife the meat should be cut in very thin, appetizingly rare and tender slices.

This is a most economical and nutritious roast, having no waste in bones and trimmings, and if cut from good beef is as delicious as a porterhouse roast.

Sauer Braten.—Rub a solid piece of the round of beef with vinegar, dust lightly with salt and pepper and a bit of bay leaf rubbed to a powder. Let the meat stand over night or twelve hours. Cut several slashes in the meat, put in two small onions cut in quarters and two carrots cut in strips and the same amount of turnip. Dust a pinch of poultry seasoning or sweet herbs over. Lay three thin slices of salt pork in the well-greased paper bag, add a half cupful boiling water and if there is room in the bag tuck in a few more carrots or onions. Seal and place in a very hot oven for eight minutes, then reduce the heat at least half, and cook about two hours. Have a dripping pan with an inch of water in it, set under the oven rack so that if by any mischance the bag should burst, nothing would be lost. The steam from the water in the pan serves the same purpose as wetting the bag before filling, keeping it from becoming too brittle. Two bags will be found better than one in this case.

Beef Steak.—Wipe the meat, trim off extra fat and brush over with oil or butter. Season lightly with salt and pepper, put in well-greased bag, seal, place on grid in very hot oven and cook from fifteen to eighteen minutes, according to thickness of steak. At the last, pierce a few holes in the top of the bag, if there is any doubt about the steak being sufficiently browned. Take up on hot platter and spread with parsley butter, pouring any gravy remaining in the pan over the meat.

Toledo Beef Steak.—Place a top sirloin steak in a wood cookery dish, season with salt and pepper and place in bag. Seal and cook twenty minutes. Remove from the oven, open the bag and turn the steak. Spread over the top a little dry mustard and season with salt, pepper, two tablespoonfuls of drawn butter and a large tablespoonful of Worcestershire sauce. Place on the top grate of the oven without the bag, and leave ten or fifteen minutes until crisp and brown.

Stuffed Roast Beef or "Mock Duck."—Take two flank steaks or one large round steak. If the former, sew together with coarse strong cotton, leaving one side open like a bag to be filled with the dressing. If the latter, place on the meat board and spread with a dressing made from mashed potato, well seasoned, sweet potatoes sliced and seasoned, or a forcemeat made from two cupfuls bread crumbs, a quarter cup butter or vegetable oil, in which a chopped onion has been cooked, with salt, pepper and cloves to season. The Germans like a half cupful of seeded raisins or chopped prunes added to this. Roll the meat about the filling and tie with strips of cotton cloth, or if you are using the flank steak, stuff the pocket and tie in shape. Butter the pocket or roll well on the outside, slip into a large well-buttered bag, add a tablespoonful of broth or hot water, seal, and cook in a hot oven ten minutes.

Reduce the heat and cook forty or fifty minutes more according to weight of the steak. A second bag over the first is advised here when the roll is heavy.

CHAPTER XI.

LAMB AND MUTTON.

THE paper bag seems made expressly for lamb and mutton cookery.

Breast of Lamb With Tomato Sauce.—Get three pounds breast of lamb, boil until tender, and slip out the bones. This is best done the day before you are to bag it. Half an hour before serving, egg, crumb, season and put in a well-greased bag. Seal and put in a very hot oven for twenty minutes. Serve with tomato sauce.

Lamb Chops.—If you use the rib chops have them frenched, saving the trimmings for the stock pot. If you have the loin chops, skewer to keep in shape. Season with salt and pepper and brush over with oil or melted butter. Put in a well-greased bag, seal, place on the grid shelf in a hot oven, and cook for ten or fifteen minutes according to the thickness of the chop. When done put on a hot platter and spread with parsley or mint butter.

Lamb or Mutton Cutlets With Tomatoes.—Cut the best end of the neck into neat cutlets, flatten and trim. Season with salt and pepper, brush with melted butter or oil, sprinkle with mint or chopped parsley and chives, and place in a buttered bag, with a tablespoonful of tomato on each chop. Seal and cook in hot oven twelve or fifteen minutes.

Lamb Fry.—Wash thoroughly a pound and a half of lamb's fry and put in a pan of cold water. Simmer five minutes, lift out and pat dry on a soft cloth. Divide in nice pieces, dip in a batter made of one egg, one tablespoonful of milk, salt and pepper to season and flour to make of the consistency of cream. Arrange these pieces in a buttered bag. Seal and bake ten minutes. Serve with fried parsley.

Lamb's Kidney.—Skin, split, dip in butter and place on skewer. Dust with salt and pepper, and place in buttered bag. Seal, place in hot oven and cook eight minutes.

Leg of Mutton Cooked in Cider.—Buy the leg of mutton two or three days before you wish to serve it. Take off the "woolly" skin that has the strong taste on the outside and wipe carefully with a damp cloth. Then rub with a mixture of spices, using half a teaspoonful each of cinnamon, cloves, allspice, pepper and nutmeg. Rub thoroughly and hang the mutton in a cool place for two days; then put in a well-greased bag, adding four onions chopped fine, a cupful seedless raisins and a cupful of sweet cider.

Put in hot oven and bake half an hour, then reduce the heat, and cook an hour and a half. Serve with a hot cider sauce.

Mutton Chops and Sausage.—Place two thick chops in a wooden dish with three links of sausage. Season lightly with salt and pepper, lay two strips of bacon over the top of the chops and seal in bag. Bake from twenty minutes to half an hour in a moderate oven.

Ragout of Lamb.—Grease the bag well, and lay in a layer of sliced raw potatoes, seasoned lightly. Put on top of the potatoes a layer of meat, seasoned with salt, pepper and chopped parsley, and lay thin slices of onion across meat. Add one-half cup canned tomato or tomato sauce, cover the whole with another layer of sliced potato, seal, and bake thirty-five minutes. You may use a wooden cooking dish here to advantage.

Roast Leg of Lamb.—Trim nicely and rub over with oil, dredge with a little flour and season with salt, pepper and powdered mint. Seal and bake two hours. Serve with mint sauce.

A Genuine Irish Stew.—Cut two pounds of chops from the best end of a neck of mutton, and pare away nearly all the fat. A portion of the breast may be cut into squares and used, but a neck of mutton is the best joint for the purpose. Take as many potatoes as will amount after peeling to twice the weight of the meat. Slice them with eight large onions sliced. Put a layer of mixed potatoes and onions at the bottom of the buttered paper bag. Place the meat on this and season it plentifully with pepper and lightly with salt. Pack closely, and cover the meat with another layer of potato and onion. Pour in as much water or stock as will moisten the topmost layer, seal tightly, and let the contents cook gently for two and a half hours. You may use one of the large wooden cooking dishes here.

CHAPTER XII.

PORK IN VARIED FORMS.

Bacon and Apples.—CORE, but do not peel, well flavored apples and cut in crosswise rings about a quarter of an inch thick. Lay on thin slices of streaky bacon in a well-buttered bag, dust lightly with sugar, seal and cook eight minutes in a hot oven.

Bacon and Bananas.—Peel firm bananas, halve them lengthwise, dust lightly with pepper and wrap each in a thin slice of streaky bacon. Put in a well-greased bag, seal and cook in a hot oven ten minutes.

Bacon and Calf's Liver.—Pour boiling water over thin slices of calf's liver and let stand ten minutes. Drain, pat dry and dredge with flour, seasoning with pepper and a little salt. Lay slices of bacon in a greased bag and on top put a layer of the liver, seal and bake fifteen minutes. Serve on hot platter.

Baked Pork Chops.—Season with salt and pepper, then cover each side of the chops with a forcemeat made moist enough to stick to them. Place in a well-greased bag, adding a spoonful of water, seal and bake twenty-five minutes.

Pork Chops and Sweet Potatoes.—Select six sweet potatoes of uniform size. Peel, cut in half lengthwise, brush each piece all over with melted butter and dredge lightly with powdered sugar. Place in a thoroughly buttered bag flat side down. On top of them put pork chops, seasoned, rolled in flour and from which the fat has been partly trimmed. Seal and bake in hot oven on broiler for twenty-five minutes.

Pork chops cooked in this way are as tender as chicken, not hard in fibre as they usually are when fried.

Ham and Scalloped Potatoes.—Peel and slice potatoes very thin. Put a layer in the bottom of a buttered bag and on top of the potatoes a layer of raw ham sliced very thin, and with the most of the fat trimmed off. Sprinkle with a little flour. Add little bits of butter rolled in flour and salt and pepper to season. Proceed in this way until the desired amount is obtained, having the top layer of potatoes sprinkled with flour and bits of butter. Turn in enough sweet milk or cream to come even with the top layer, and bake twenty minutes or until the potatoes are tender. The trimmings from the fat of the ham can be used in place of the butter if preferred. One of the wooden cooking dishes is convenient here.

Ham, Spinach and Lamb Chops.—Place two or more slices of ham in a wood cookery dish. Spread over it the contents of a small can of spinach and on top of the spinach place Frenched lamb chops. Put in greased paper bag, and surround by six potatoes prepared for baking. Close the bag, and bake 45 minutes in a moderate oven. This makes a very easy dinner—as the whole meal can be cooked in the oven without having to be watched—and the mistress of the house can be ready dressed to entertain guests without danger of spoiling her frock by spattering grease.

Stuffed Fresh Ham or Shoulder.—Have the knuckle and bone removed, wash, wipe dry, season with salt and pepper and fill the bone space with a forcemeat to which apples or stewed prunes have been added. Sew or skewer into shape, then lay skin side up in a large, well-greased bag. Add a half cup of water or cider, a few slices of onion, seal and bake for fifteen minutes in a very hot oven, then reduce the heat one-half and bake an hour.

Roast Loin of Pork.—Sprinkle with salt and pepper, dredge lightly with flour and put into a greased bag with a half cup of water or tomato. Seal and bake an hour and a half. Serve with apples baked in another bag.

Roast Spare-Rib.—Cut the skin of the spare-rib in checks, season with salt and pepper and put in a well-greased bag surrounded by apples or sweet potatoes cut in halves, and bake three-quarters of an hour.

Baked Sausage With Apples.—Put links of sausage or sausage cakes in greased bag, and surround with well flavored apples cored and cut in halves but not peeled. Stand the apples flesh side down. Seal and bake fifteen minutes.

Baked Sausage and Potato.—Get the best country sausage meat and mould into a little roll. Dust lightly with flour and put into a well-greased bag. Peel enough potatoes to make a wall about the meat and cut them in halves. They should stand with the cut side against the meat. Seal the bag and bake about thirty minutes until the potatoes are tender and brown and the sausage well done. If desired, use the drippings that come from the sausage as the foundation for a cream gravy to serve with the sausage or serve without. Sausage cooked in this way is also nice sliced cold and makes appetizing sandwiches for the school lunch basket.

Baked Sausage With Toast.—Put a half dozen link sausages in a well-greased bag, separating them by as many slices of bread cut the same height. Add a half cup of good brown sauce and a few mushrooms if desired. Seal and bake twelve minutes. Serve with the sauce and a little minced parsley sprinkled over the sausage.

Baked Sausage With Tomatoes.—Put into the greased bag sausage cakes or links. Chop fine one small onion, a teaspoonful of parsley and two tomatoes, spread over the sausage, seal and cook twenty minutes.

Tenderloin of Pork.—Get fat, large tenderloins and have them split, but leave connected down the side. Fill with a good forcemeat or potato dressing well seasoned, skewer the edges together or tie with string, put in well-greased bag adding a tablespoonful of water and bake twenty minutes. Serve with curried apples, made in this way and baked in another bag at the same time. Peel and core the apples and fill the cavities with a mixture of curry powder, grated cheese and fine breadcrumbs. For eight apples use four tablespoonfuls and a half of curry powder and eight of the bread crumbs. Moisten the mixture with milk. Bag, seal and bake. These apples are nice served cold with cold roast pork.

CHAPTER XIII.

VEAL.

Baked Calf's Liver.—ONE calf's liver washed and dried, slashed and scored inside. Have bread dressing ready well seasoned with onions. Stuff the liver with this and tie with cord. Skewer to liver with toothpicks several pieces of bacon, put a little hot water in the bag and bake at least one hour in a hot oven. Send to table hot, with a parsley garnish.

Calves' Brains in Tempting But Inexpensive Ways.—Carefully prepared few can tell the difference between sweetbreads and calves' brains though the housewife will appreciate the fact that sweetbreads cost about four times as much as the brains. In whichever way one elects to cook the brains, the preliminary treatment is the same. Parboil fifteen minutes in water, to which has been added a teaspoonful of salt and a tablespoonful of vinegar. After this, let them lie in cold water a few moments, then remove all membranes and dark streaks. They are now ready to be cooked in any way preferred.

Breaded Brains.—Separate the lobes of a pair of brains that have been parboiled as directed. Then with a sharp knife split each division. Beat the yolk of an egg lightly, thin slightly with cold water or milk, dip the brains in this, then into finely rolled crumbs. Put in a buttered bag and bake twenty minutes. Serve on a hot dish with a garnish of quarters of lemon that have been rolled in finely minced parsley.

Sweetbreads.—The initial treatment of sweetbreads, when they come from the market, is always the same. Parboil at once in salted water, from fifteen to thirty minutes, never allowing them to boil. Then plunge into ice water and lemon juice or vinegar (a tablespoonful to a quart of water) and leave for an hour to blanch and become firm. After parboiling, the little strings and membranes can be very readily removed. Now they are ready for the finishing culinary touch, in anyway the cook may elect.

Baked Sweetbreads.—Sprinkle with salt and pepper, roll in crumbs then beaten egg to which a spoonful of milk has been added, then in crumbs again, the last time having the crumbs well-buttered. Put in greased bag and bake half an hour in a moderately hot oven. Serve on toast with the brown gravy poured over the slices.

Sweetbreads With Bacon.—Slice sweetbreads, roll in seasoned crumbs, then in egg and again in crumbs. Put on a skewer, alternating with slices of bacon cut thin, put in a greased bag, and bake twenty minutes in medium oven.

Larded Sweetbreads.—Lard the boiled sweetbreads with strips of bacon and lemon peel, having the bacon in the centre and peel on the sides. Lay in paper bag with brown gravy to half cover, and let them bake for an hour, or until brown. Arrange on a hot dish, thicken the gravy with a little flour and season with catsup, lemon juice and spices to taste. Pour over the sweetbreads and serve with peas.

Sweetbreads Straight.—Parboil the sweetbreads, take off the skins, dust each sweetbread with salt and pepper very lightly and pour over each a tablespoonful of cream. Slip the sweetbreads into a thickly greased bag and cook in a moderate oven slowly for forty minutes. Serve on a hot dish with a border of asparagus or green peas.

Vealettes.—Purchase veal cuts from the leg in slices as large as one's hand and about half an inch thick. On each slice lay a large tablespoonful of dressing made from seasoned bread crumbs, a beaten egg and a tablespoonful of melted butter. Roll up the slices, pinning with toothpicks to keep the dressing in. Put in a well-greased bag, seal and bake about three-quarters of an hour. When done, thicken the gravy, pour over the veal and serve on a hot platter.

A variation in vealettes is made by getting from the butcher two slices of veal and a slice of ham the same size. Put together like a sandwich with the ham in the center and skewer together. Trim the edges evenly and bake in a bag. When the veal is done take up on a hot platter, thicken the drippings remaining in the bag, adding enough hot water to make a good consistency.

Veal Loaf.—Mince three pounds raw lean veal and a quarter pound of fine fat pork, salt or fresh. Season with half an onion, grated fine, a tablespoonful of salt, a half teaspoonful of pepper, a half teaspoonful powdered thyme, quarter of a spoonful sweet marjoram, the same amount Summer savory and a saltspoonful celery salt. Next mix in two-thirds of a cup of rolled cracker crumbs, a scant cupful veal gravy or hot milk, the yolk of one egg and the whites of two beaten together until light. Mix thoroughly and form into a compact loaf. Roll it until coated in yolks of the two eggs left over, then in sifted cracker or bread crumbs, and put in buttered bag and bake in a moderate oven. Roast two hours and serve cold, cut in very thin slices.

Shoulder of Veal Stuffed and Braised.—Buy a shoulder of veal and ask the butcher to bone it and send the bones with the meat. Cover the bones with cold water and when it comes to a boil, skim, then add a little onion and carrot, a few seasoning herbs and any spices desired. Simmer gently for an hour or so until you have a pint of stock. To make the stuffing, take a stale loaf, cut off the crust and soak in a little cold water until soft. Rub the crumb of the loaf as fine as possible in the hands, then add to the soaked and softened crust. Chop a half cupful of suet fine, put into a frying pan a tablespoonful of the suet, and when hot add an onion chopped fine. Cook until brown, then add to the bread with regular poultry seasoning or else salt, pepper and a bit of thyme. Mix well and stuff the cavity in the shoulder, then pull the flaps of the meat over and sew up. Put the rest of the suet in the frying pan, and having dusted the meat with flour, salt, pepper and a sprinkling of sugar, brown on all sides in the fat. Into the bottom of the bag put a layer of thin sliced onion and carrot, a bit of bay leaf and sprigs of parsley, and on this lay the meat. Add two or three cloves, pour the hot stock around it, cover closely and braise in a hot oven for two and a half hours.

CHAPTER XIV.

SAUCES AND GRAVIES.

Bignon's Sauce.—THIS is a delightful appetizer with meats cold or hot, or with fish. Chop fine equal parts, say one tablespoonful of each, capers, parsley, chives, gherkins, tarragon and green Chili peppers. Mix together; season with salt, pepper and cayenne and cover with tarragon vinegar; let it stand an hour and add three tablespoonfuls of oil and a teaspoonful of French mustard.

Bread Sauce.—Mince an onion and boil in milk until soft. Then strain the milk over one cupful of grated bread crumbs and stand aside, closely covered, for an hour. Add the minced onion, two tablespoonfuls of butter, pepper, salt and a bit of mace to season. Set over the fire, boil up and serve with roasted or broiled birds.

Brown Sauce.—The formula for this is the same as for the white sauce, except that the butter and fat are browned before the flour is added, or browned flour is used for thickening. Use a little more flour proportionately, in a brown sauce, as the browning destroys, in a measure, the thickening qualities of the flour. Reduce with brown stock or water.

With this as foundation, any number of palatable sauces can be invented which will be found useful in disposing of many odds and ends of vegetables, cold meats and left-over fish, that might otherwise "go begging."

Celery Sauce.—Prepare a smooth, white sauce by blending over the fire two tablespoonfuls each butter, and flour, then reducing with a pint of warm milk. Add a dozen stalks of celery that have been minced fine and cooked tender in just enough water to cover. Cook two minutes, season with salt and pepper and serve with boiled fowl.

Currant Jelly Sauce.—This makes a delicious addition to roast venison or mutton. Cook together in a saucepan one tablespoonful butter and a teaspoonful minced onion. When the onion is lightly colored, (not blackened) add a teaspoonful of flour and stir until smooth. Add gradually a half cupful stock, stirring all the time, and when it boils up add a bit of bay leaf, a teaspoonful vinegar, a half teaspoonful salt, and eighth teaspoonful pepper, one clove, and a tablespoonful of currant jelly. Simmer five minutes, strain and serve hot.

Curry Sauce.—This is nice with any delicate meat or fish or can be poured over boiled rice for a side dish. Put two tablespoonfuls butter in a saucepan, then stir into it two tablespoonfuls flour. Add a scant tablespoonful curry powder and a teaspoonful onion juice, and cook a moment or two, but do not allow them to brown. Stir in gradually one cupful milk and cook until smooth and thickened. Add a cup of cream, season with salt and just before serving, add, if you like, a hard boiled egg chopped fine.

Hollandaise Sauce.—Put one-half cup of butter into a bowl of cold water and wash it to take out the salt. Divide it into three parts and put one-third into the top of a double boiler with the yolks of two eggs and a tablespoon of lemon juice. Stir and cook until the butter melts, add another piece of butter and continue stirring. As the sauce thickens stir in the last piece, add one-third cup of boiling water, a speck of cayenne and a saltspoon of salt and cook one minute.

Horseradish Sauce.—Put a saucepan over the fire with a tablespoonful of butter and a half tablespoonful of flour. Stir and cook two minutes, then add a half cupful of strained soup stock and a half cupful of milk, six whole peppers, a bit of bay leaf and an even half teaspoonful of salt. Cook five minutes, remove bay leaf and peppers, and add three tablespoonfuls grated horseradish. Cook two minutes and serve.

Maitre d'Hotel Butter.—To make it, rub a quarter cupful of butter to a cream, add a half teaspoonful of salt, a good dash of pepper, white or paprika, a tablespoonful of fine chopped parsley and a tablespoonful of lemon juice. If you are partial to nutmeg, a grating of that is sometimes added.

Mexican Sauce.—Take four large tomatoes or the equivalent in canned, three green peppers and one onion. Chop pepper and onion in a wooden bowl, add the tomato and salt and pepper to season. To one-half cupful of vinegar, add the drippings from four slices fried bacon, pour over the chopped vegetables and serve in individual salad dishes as an accompaniment to meats.

Mint Sauce for Roast Lamb.—Put one cup of vinegar and one rounding tablespoon of sugar together and stir in one-quarter cup of finely minced mint. Let stand fifteen minutes before it is served.

French Mustard Sauce, Creole Style.—Work together three tablespoonfuls mustard and one cupful sugar, then beat in one egg until smooth. Add one cupful of vinegar a little at a time, set over the fire and cook three or four minutes stirring constantly. When cold add one tablespoonful olive oil beating all well together.

An Excellent Mustard Sauce for Cold Meat.—Two teaspoonfuls flour, one teaspoonful sugar, one teaspoonful mustard, a little pepper and salt. Mash all together, add boiling water, to make thick paste. Beat constantly till lumps are all out. Add sufficient vinegar to make it thinner. Be sure the water is boiling.

Onion Sauce.—Prepare a smooth white sauce by blending over the fire two tablespoonfuls of butter and a tablespoonful and a half of flour. When bubbly, turn in two cupfuls of hot milk, and stir until smooth and thickened. Add two large boiled onions minced fine, cook a moment, season with salt and pepper and serve with poultry or boiled veal.

Spanish Sauce.—For veal, lamb or mutton chops, broiled or fried fish, chicken, etc. One large onion, one full section of garlic, one-half large sweet, green or red pepper. Put in two tablespoonfuls of butter, one teaspoonful of olive or vegetable oil. When effervescing stops add a half teaspoonful of salt, and the onion, garlic and green pepper which has been finely grated. When this begins to brown, giving it time to cook rather well, add four good sized tomatoes, skinned and chopped, or the thick part of one can of tomatoes. Let all simmer for fifteen to twenty minutes with occasional stirring to prevent burning. Add salt and pepper, paprika, or cayenne to taste, two tablespoonfuls tomato ketchup and one dessertspoonful Worcestershire Sauce, before taking off fire. It should be the consistency of good cream. If too thin, cook down, or if too thick add a sufficient amount of *boiling* water. Use red pepper as a seasoning.

Thick Tomato Sauce.—Blend over the fire two tablespoonfuls of melted butter and two tablespoonfuls of flour; add a little at a time, and stirring all the while, one large cupful of tomato juice. Stir until the mixture thickens; then season to taste with sugar, salt and cayenne pepper. The seasoning may sometimes be varied by adding a little chopped parsley or chopped onion or even both. For a thinner tomato sauce—use but one tablespoonful of butter and one of flour to each cupful of liquor.

Sauce Tartare.—Make first a good mayonnaise, then finish with the addition of a tablespoonful each of chopped gherkins, olives, parsley and capers; mix together in a bowl a half teaspoonful of salt, a half teaspoonful mustard, a half teaspoonful of powdered sugar and a half saltspoonful of pepper; add the yolks of two raw eggs that have been in the ice box long enough to be as cold as possible and beat lightly; measure out a half cupful of olive oil and have this cold also; add the oil slowly at first, then as it begins to thicken it can be poured in more rapidly. When quite thick, add three tablespoonfuls of vinegar, then the chopped ingredients. This will keep several weeks. Tarragon vinegar may be used in place of the cider vinegar if preferred.

CHAPTER XV.

RECOOKED DISHES.

Beef Steak Left Overs.—MINCE fine and for each cup of meat add a tablespoonful of chopped ham and half as much bread crumbs as you have meat. Moisten the crumbs with a little hot milk and add to the meat. Season highly with salt, pepper and chopped parsley or substitute a little sage or onion juice for the parsley. Beat one egg light and add to the other ingredients. Make into a brick shaped loaf, grease over with warmed butter or oil, put in paper bag also greased. Seal and bake twenty-five minutes. Dish on a hot platter, pour tomato sauce about it or serve with horse radish sauce.

Chicken Croquettes.—To one solid cupful of meat chopped as fine as powder, add one half teaspoonful of salt, and a half saltspoonful of white pepper. Make a pint of thick cream sauce, allowing to two level tablespoonfuls of butter, two heaping tablespoonfuls of cornstarch cooked together diluted with a pint of hot milk or cream and stirred and cooked until smooth and thick. Season with salt and pepper and add enough to the chicken to make stiff enough to handle when cold. When cold shape into balls, roll in fine, dry bread crumbs and beaten egg diluted with a little water, then crumb again and place in well-greased bag. Seal and cook ten minutes.

Mock Fried Oysters.—To two cupfuls cold boiled rice, add one tin of sardines, from which all bone and skin have been removed. Roll this coarse paste into flat, circular cakes, put into well-greased bag and bake fifteen minutes in moderate oven.

Turkey Croquettes.—Chop the fragments of turkey or other left over meats very fine, adding for seasoning a small portion of bologna, ham or tongue together with a bit of fine minced onion or onion juice, salt, pepper and parsley. Make a thick cream sauce, allowing for a pint of the chopped and seasoned meat the following portions:

Put into a saucepan a heaping tablespoonful butter and two level tablespoonfuls of flour. As soon as blended, pour in a cupful of hot milk stirring until thick and smooth. Salt to taste. Add the meat and beat until well mixed.

Season more highly if desired, then set away in a cold place until cold and stiffened. Form into cones. Dip in beaten egg, roll in fine crumbs and place in a cold place again until quite dry. Bake in well-greased bag and stick a little sprig of parsley in the end of each cone before serving.

Edinboro Hot Pot.—You will need for this one pound of cold meat sliced and browned in sweet drippings, one large onion sliced and browned in the same drippings, a half tin of tomatoes, a half dozen cold boiled or baked potatoes sliced and a little good stock made from the bones and seasoning. Put a layer of meat in the well-greased bag or in one of the oval wood cookery dishes made specially for the purpose. On top of the meat put some of the onions, tomatoes and potatoes. Season with salt, pepper and butter or vegetable shortening and pour over all about a cupful of good stock. Seal the bag and bake for a half hour in a moderate oven.

Individual Meat Pies.—Chop fine any cold cooked meat. Season highly with mustard, pepper sauce and catsup, salt and pepper; add one egg; moisten with liquor of oysters. Make a rich biscuit crust, roll out to a quarter of an inch thickness, and cut in squares. Fill half of each square with one tablespoonful of the prepared meat. Fold remaining half of square over, first moistening edges with oyster liquor, and press closely together. Put in buttered bag and bake twenty minutes in hot oven, reducing the heat after the first ten minutes.

English Pasties.—Cut any cold meat up into small pieces, add a cupful of sliced potatoes, raw, and an onion chopped fine, some parsley and pepper and salt to taste. Stew this until the potato is done and thicken with flour rubbed in butter. Make a crust of flour and salt, using chopped suet and butter in equal quantities for shortening and a teaspoonful of baking powder to each quart of flour. Roll the crust out thin and cut into large discs—the cover of a two quart pail makes a good pastie cutter. Put two large spoonfuls of the meat mixture on the crust and roll over, pinching edges together like a fruit turnover. Bag and bake one-half hour in a hot oven. If there is any of the meat gravy left serve it with the pasties.

Olla Podrida Pie.—Grease one of the oval wood dishes and line with a crust about a quarter of an inch thick. Fill with meat scraps of any sort cut small and heated together in a little stock or gravy, well seasoned with tomato and powdered herbs. Small leftovers of any vegetable, peas, corn or cauliflower may also be minced and added with good effect. Cover with strips of good paste lattice fashion, slip into a well-greased bag and cook half an hour in a moderate oven.

Oyster Bundles.—Cut generous, uniform slices of cold turkey or veal, lay a slice of bacon on each, then an oyster on each slice of the bacon. Roll the three together, fasten with tooth picks and put in buttered bag. Bake fifteen minutes and serve with potatoes baked in another bag.

CHAPTER XVI.

CHEESE AND EGG DISHES.

Cheese Ball With Tomato Sauce.—MIX together two cupfuls grated cheese, a cupful of fine bread crumbs, a quarter teaspoonful of salt and a few grains of cayenne. Then add two eggs beaten stiff, shape in small balls, roll in crushed cracker crumbs and lay in well-buttered bag. Bake ten minutes and serve on triangles of buttered toast with tomato sauce.

Cheese Fritters to Serve With the Salad Course.—Beat two eggs, season with salt, pepper and a suspicion of mustard and then lay in this seasoned egg as many thin slices of American cheese as it will hold. Have ready tart apples cored and sliced crosswise without peeling. Put a slice of cheese between two rounds of apple, sandwich fashion, dip the sandwiches in the egg, lay in a well-greased paper bag seal and cook ten minutes. Serve very hot.

Pepper Cheese.—Take green peppers, scorch slightly in hot oven or over the coals, then remove the outer skin with a sharp knife. Split the peppers, remove the seeds, and put in their place a small roll of cream cheese. Roll up again, skewer together with a wooden tooth-pick, dip in beaten egg and cracker crumbs and put in well-buttered bag. Seal and bake fifteen minutes in hot oven.

Cheese Ramekins.—Roll out a sheet of pie crust and sprinkle liberally with grated cheese. Roll up and roll out again. Sprinkle on more cheese and repeat the rolling. Stamp out with a biscuit cutter (the pastry should be about a quarter of an inch thick), put in buttered bag and bake in a hot oven. When done, dip both sides in melted butter and serve hot.

Cheese and Eggs.—Butter the bottom of a baking dish and cover with slices of rich cheese. Break several whole eggs over the cheese, taking care that the whites and yolks do not become separated. Season with salt and pepper, and pour over all a rich cream, a half tablespoonful to each egg.

Baked Eggs.—Butter little casseroles or gem pans, and drop an egg in each. Season with salt and pepper and put a little cream on the top of each egg. Put in bag, seal and bake five minutes. These are exceedingly delicate, as the steam being retained they bake quickly, yet do not become hard. Set each on a plate for serving.

Baked Eggs With Cheese.—Break into a buttered pan the number of eggs required. Pour over each one tablespoon of rich, sweet cream, sprinkle over all a thin layer of grated cheese and a few fine rolled crumbs. Season with salt and pepper, put in bag, seal, and bake about six minutes.

A Paper Bag Omelette.—Beat two eggs for about five minutes. Add a dash of salt and pepper and a heaping teaspoonful of flour. Beat again until flour is well mixed in and add a small cupful of milk. Put a tablespoonful of minced breakfast bacon into a pie tin, when quite hot pour egg mixture over it. Put in paper bag, seal, and bake a delicate brown in a quick oven. Cut in squares and serve immediately.

Cheese Omelette.—A savory of cheese omelette may be made from one egg if the following recipe is used. Soak one small cupful grated bread crumbs in two cupfuls of sweet milk into which a pinch of soda has been dissolved. Beat one egg very light and add to the softened bread. Stir in one teaspoonful of melted butter and a dash of cayenne. Beat the whole well, add a small cupful grated cheese and a teaspoonful of salt. Beat again, turn into a buttered bag, bake twenty minutes and serve at once.

Swiss Eggs.—For Swiss eggs spread the bottom of a bag with two ounces of fine American cheese. Place four eggs on the cheese, taking care that the yolks are not broken. Season with pepper and salt. Pour around the eggs two tablespoonfuls of rich cream and cover the top with grated cheese. Put in bag, seal and bake for ten minutes. Garnish with parsley and serve with fingers of crisp toast.

Eggs in Tomato Cups.—Cut fresh tomatoes in half and scoop out part of the interior. Fry the tomato cups until half done. Then break into each of them an egg. Put then in a buttered bag, seal and cook ten minutes. The tops of the eggs may be sprinkled with minced ham or grated cheese, or they may be served plain. Season and serve hot.

CHAPTER XVII.

VEGETABLES.

WHILE no claim is made that all vegetables are improved through paper bag cookery, experiments prove that quite a number can be successfully cooked by the paper bag process. Vegetables of strong flavor as a rule are best cooked in a large quantity of water and are not recommended for paper bag cookery; only the more delicate vegetables that need to have their flavors conserved. Dried peas, lentils and beans are excellent cooked in paper bags but require a longer preliminary soaking than is usual with other methods of cooking.

Asparagus.—Trim and scrape as for boiling; wash very clean. Tie in bundles and put into a buttered bag with a little salt and a quarter cupful of water. Seal and cook from thirty-five to forty minutes in a hot oven.

Asparagus With Cheese.—Boil two bunches of asparagus twelve minutes in salted water. Drain, but save the water. Put the asparagus in a buttered bag or in one of the oval wooden dishes, scattering grated Swiss or Parmesan cheese between the layers. Turn over all a cup of the water in which the asparagus was boiled, sprinkle the top of the scallop with a little cheese and a few buttered bread crumbs. Seal the bag and cook fifteen minutes in a moderate oven.

Lima Beans.—Add to a quart of shelled Lima beans three tablespoonfuls of butter or vegetable oil, a quarter pound of diced bacon or ham, a little minced parsley or other seasoning herbs, and a teaspoonful of flour. Put in a greased bag with a cupful of water, seal and cook an hour in a moderate oven.

String Beans, Oriental Style.—String the beans, cut in two lengthwise, then break in inch pieces. To every pint of beans, which should be young and tender, allow one cupful boiling water, two tablespoonfuls vegetable oil, one small onion sliced, and a half cupful tomato. Salt and pepper to taste. Put all in greased paper bag and cook forty-five minutes. A wooden cookery dish can be employed to advantage.

Boston Baked Bean Cakes.—These are made of left-over baked beans. Heat with a little water to moisten, rub through a colander, season with salt, pepper and mustard. Put a tablespoonful of pork drippings or butter in a frying pan, and cook in it, when hot, a tablespoonful of minced onion, taking care not to let it blacken. Add to the beans, make into cakes and lay in well-greased bag. Cook twenty minutes and serve with tomato sauce.

Bean Croquettes.—Soak one pint white pea beans or the little brown Mexican frijoles over night in cold water. In the morning cook until soft in water to which a saltspoonful of soda has been added, changing the water after it first comes to a boil. Rub through a colander, then add to the pulp one cup grated bread crumbs, one tablespoonful minced parsley, two tablespoonfuls melted butter, two eggs well beaten, one small onion grated and salt and pepper to season. Mix thoroughly, shape into cylinders, dip in beaten egg, then in cracker dust and put in buttered bag. Seal and cook ten minutes in hot oven.

German Cabbage.—Take two small hard heads of red cabbage and cut in slices half an inch thick, discarding the hard stalk and veins. Put onto a greased wooden cookery bowl two rounding tablespoonfuls of melted butter or vegetable oil, then add the cabbage, sprinkle with a level teaspoonful of salt, three tablespoonfuls of vinegar and one onion chopped fine. Put in bag, seal, and put in oven. Bake one hour with only one burner on after the first ten minutes.

Cabbage Hot Slaw.—Chop a small hard head of cabbage fine and salt it lightly. Let stand half an hour then put in wooden bowl with two tablespoonfuls of butter. Put in bag, seal, and cook slowly in the oven for twenty minutes. No water is necessary, as the salt will draw out the juices of the cabbage so it will have moisture enough. At the end of twenty minutes take up with a hot dish, add a teaspoonful of flour that has been stirred in a little cold water, then cooked until thick with a half cupful of cream. Lastly, add one tablespoonful of pure vinegar and serve at once.

Carrots.—Wash and scrape a half dozen tender carrots. Slice thin and season with salt, pepper and a good tablespoonful of butter. Add a half cupful good stock, put in a well-greased bag, seal and cook thirty-five minutes.

Carrot Saute.—Scrape and cook young carrots in boiling salted water until tender. Cut in halves lengthwise, roll in fine cracker crumbs, then in egg and cracker again, and put in well-greased bag. Bake fifteen minutes, sprinkle with fine chopped parsley and serve very hot.

Stuffed Eggplant.—Select purple fruit and of small size. Halve them, sprinkle them with salt, turn them cut side down on a fine sieve, put a heavy plate on them and let them drain for an hour. Wipe dry, take from each a tablespoonful of the center, chop it fine and for each tablespoonful allow the same amount of bread crumbs, a teaspoonful of chopped onions, olives and vegetable oil, with a little salt and a dusting of paprika. Mound this dressing on each half, arrange the halves in a buttered bag, pour in water to the depth of an inch, add a generous piece of butter, salt and pepper, and place the bag in a hot oven; twenty minutes should be sufficiently long to cook the eggplant thoroughly.

Lentil Cutlets.—Soak one cupful dried lentils all night with a cupful dried lima beans. In the morning drain, add two quarts of water, a stalk of celery and half an onion sliced. Cook until soft, remove the seasonings and rub through a puree sieve. Add one cupful stale bread crumbs, one beaten egg, the juice of a half lemon and seasonings to taste. Melt a heaping tablespoonful of butter in a small saucepan, add to it a tablespoonful flour and pour on, when blended, a third of a cup of milk. Let the mixture cook until thick and smooth, then add to the lentil mixture and set aside to cool. Shape into small cutlets, dip in beaten egg, then in fine cracker crumb, put in a well-buttered bag and bake twenty minutes. Serve with a tomato sauce.

Mushrooms.—Choose fine fat mushrooms, cut the stem close, peel and wipe delicately with a damp cloth. Sprinkle lightly with salt and lay in a well-greased bag together with a big tablespoonful of butter rolled in flour and a half cupful of rich cream. Seal and cook twelve minutes in a hot oven.

Baked Onions.—Parboil for fifteen minutes Bermuda or Spanish onions, chill in cold water, then if very large cut in halves, otherwise, cut a little wedge out of the hearts and fill the cavity with butter or vegetable oil. Put in the well-greased bag, adding a little water and more butter or oil, seal and cook twenty minutes.

Stuffed Baked Onions.—The next time you have a roast leg of lamb or mutton, try baked onions prepared in this way as an accompaniment: Take large onions, preferably Spanish or Bermudas, peel, cut a slice from the top of each, and with a small spoon scoop out about half the pulp. Put this in a dish, mix with it an equal quantity of bread crumbs, well flavored with chopped parsley, sweet marjoram, salt and pepper. Moisten the whole lightly with cream and a little melted butter; mix well, fill the onion cavities with the stuffing, crown with a slice of bacon for a cover, put in a bag and bake one hour in a moderate oven.

Onions With Cheese.—Skin large Spanish onions and boil until quite soft. Press through a sieve and put into a well-buttered wooden baking dish. Season with salt, pepper and plenty of butter, add a little stock or milk, grate a little cheese over them, put in bag and bake to a golden brown.

Parsnips.—Scrape and parboil some parsnips. Cut in two lengthwise. Season with pepper and salt, roll in melted butter, dripping or olive oil.

Flour again and place in a well-greased paper bag. Seal up and bake in a hot oven on a wire rack for half an hour. They should be a golden brown.

Green Peas.—Shell the peas, put into a well-buttered bag with a little salt to season, a little sprig of green mint and a half cupful of water. Seal and cook twenty-five minutes. Slit open the bag, pour its contents into a hot dish, season well with butter and serve.

Stuffed Peppers.—In preparing peppers for stuffing, select those of uniform size, wash and plunge in boiling water for about ten minutes; then drop into cold water to keep them green; cut off the stem ends and scoop out the seeds and inside of the peppers; fill with any of the following stuffings or a combination of your own devising.

Stuffing No. 1. Wash half a cup of rice; cover with boiling water and cook rapidly for ten minutes; then turn into a sieve to drain. Peel three large tomatoes, removing the seeds and cutting the pulp in small pieces. When fresh tomatoes are out of season, their equivalent in canned may be used. Mix the rice and tomatoes together; add two tablespoonfuls of olive oil or melted butter and season with salt. Fill the drained peppers with the mixture, sprinkling a few buttered crumbs over the top and replace the covers. Oil the peppers on the outside, and set in a buttered bag. Turn enough stock into the bag to come half way up the sides of the peppers (if you have no stock use hot water in which a tablespoonful of kitchen bouquet has been dissolved and several slices of onion and carrot added), and bake in a moderate oven three-quarters of an hour. Rice that has been left over from dinner may be used, leaving the tomatoes out and seasoning with chopped celery, parsley, salt and pepper. When done, dish on a hot platter and pour a rich brown sauce over them, scattering a little minced parsley over the top. A wooden cookery dish is advised here.

Stuffing No. 2. For eight good sized peppers take a pint of chopped meat, veal or chicken, or veal mixed with sausage, a cupful of soft bread crumbs and a cup of stock, gravy or water in which a spoonful of beef extract has been dissolved. Season with an even teaspoonful each of salt and pepper and half teaspoonful each summer savory, thyme and sage. Mix well, fill the peppers, sprinkle fine buttered bread crumbs over them at the end where the stuffing is exposed, put in a buttered bag and bake until well browned. This will take about a quarter of an hour. Serve with chicken or roast beef, and with or without a sauce.

Peppers With Creamed Fish.—Parboil the peppers ten minutes, then fill with creamed fish of any kind, which may be seasoned with a tablespoonful of sherry. Then sprinkle with a layer of fine crumbs, dot with butter, bag, and brown lightly in a quick oven. Creamed carrots, cauliflower, sprouts, and many other vegetables may be baked in the pepper cups and served either as a vegetable or an entree. Filled with potatoes au gratin and browned they are a delicious accompaniment for chops and steaks.

Baked Irish Potatoes.—Scrub thoroughly and rinse as many good sized potatoes as will be required. Make a few slits in them but do not peel. Place in the paper bag with a tablespoonful of water, close tightly and cook from thirty-five to fifty minutes, according to size.

Baked Potatoes Without Their Coats or Jackets.—Select as many potatoes of the same size as desired. Peel and let them stand in salted, cold water for ten minutes. Then drain without drying and place in a greased bag,—bacon fat is good for these potatoes—and cook in a hot oven, without disturbing, for forty-five minutes if small, one hour, if large. They will have a crisp, brown coat, every part of which can be eaten.

Potatoes en Surprise.—Choose potatoes of smooth shape, not too large and of even size. Scrape out from the top of each a space large enough to hold the yolk of an egg. Salt and pepper the nest, drop in a tiny bit of butter, then the egg yolk, follow with a thin slice of bacon just large enough to cover the egg and set in greased paper bag. If necessary to keep them upright cut a thin slice from the bottom of each potato, add a spoonful of cold water, seal, set in a hot oven and cook for thirty minutes.

Potatoes Farci.—A new and very delicious way of serving stuffed potatoes is as follows: Wash large potatoes and bake in bag until nearly done; take from the oven and nearly cut off one end, leaving the skin for a hinge and a bit of potato for a lid. Pull out the undone heart with a fork and in its place lay shavings of smoked bacon, peppered and tightly rolled after having been laid for an instant on a hot frying pan; close the potato and set in the oven to finish cooking.

Sauer Kraut.—Put enough to serve six people in one of the largest size wood cookery dishes, salt and season to taste, add a half cupful of water, put in bag, seal, and bake one hour in moderate oven.

Waldorf Sauer Kraut.—Soak the sauer kraut in cold water until just palatably salt. Put into greased paper bag on a wooden cookery dish with a little bacon, pickled pork or sausage, add a half cupful of hot water and cook about twenty minutes. Drain, put in a hot dish with or without the meat as desired and serve. When boiled sauer kraut is cold it may be chopped and reheated in a buttered bag with butter, gravy or a white sauce.

Sweet Potatoes and Bacon.—Peel boiled sweet potatoes, fasten a slice of bacon around each, using a wooden tooth pick to hold in place. Put in buttered bag with a spoonful of water, and bake ten minutes.

Sweet Potato Straws.—Cut potatoes in slices lengthwise, peel, then cut into straws. Dip in bacon fat or melted butter, put in buttered bag, seal, and cook fifteen minutes. Take out on soft paper to absorb any grease, dust lightly with salt and serve.

Sweet Potato en Brochette.—Peel and cut in half inch, uniform slices. Put on skewers in groups of four, place in boiling water and parboil ten minutes. Drain, brush over with vegetable oil, sprinkle with brown sugar, put in greased bag and bake twenty minutes in moderate oven.

Spinach.—Pick over carefully, thoroughly wash, then put into a bag, leaving the vegetable quite damp. Add a little salt, seal and cook thirty minutes. Before lifting the bag from the oven slide a pan under it, and prick the bottom of the bag so the water will drain out. Dish, adding butter to season and serve.

Summer Squash in Butter.—Cut into narrow strips and season with salt and pepper. Put into well-greased bag, add a generous lump of butter and cook about half an hour.

Stuffed Summer Squash.—Boil in lightly salted water until tender. Cut off the top and scoop out the inside. Mix well with seasoned and buttered crumbs, chopped onion and grated cheese. Fill the shell, sprinkle the top with buttered crumbs, put in bag and bake until brown.

Stuffed Tomatoes With Cream.—Mix together three-quarters of a cupful of cold-chopped chicken or veal, three tablespoonfuls of soft bread crumbs, a tablespoonful of melted butter, one teaspoonful of chopped parsley, half a teaspoonful of salt and quarter teaspoonful of paprika. Wash and wipe six medium-sized tomatoes, take a small piece from the stem end, carefully remove a portion of the pulp, and fill the hole with the stuffing; place in a buttered bag and cook for thirty minutes in a moderate oven. Remove to a hot platter, whip three tablespoonfuls of rich cream, add to it two tablespoonfuls of melted butter, and pour a small portion over each tomato.

Turnips.—Peel and slice your turnips and put them in a well-greased bag with a light seasoning of salt, a lump of butter barely dusted with flour, and enough thin stock to half cover them. Seal and cook in a moderate oven for an hour more or less according to the tenderness of the vegetable. Empty into a hot dish and if not rich enough add more butter, and dust with black pepper and salt.

Turnip Balls.—Peel fine grained turnips, then cut into balls, using a vegetable scoop. Put into a well-greased bag with a light seasoning of salt, a little sugar, a dusting of pepper, a tablespoonful of butter or vegetable oil and a quarter cupful of hot water, seal, and cook half an hour until tender, but not brown. Take up, add a half cupful hot cream sauce, stir lightly in it, sprinkle with minced parsley and serve very hot.

Stuffed Vine Leaves or Dolmas.—Choose tender vine leaves and scald them, after which roll a little of the following stuffing in each leaf, making it round and firm so that the stuffing will not come out when the balls are boiled. Chop three onions, put a teacupful of good salad oil in a stewing-pan, and, when it is boiling hot, throw in the chopped onion. As soon as this begins to cook, add a small cupful of Carolina rice, some chopped parsley and mint, salt and pepper and a tablespoonful of currants and mix well on the fire till the rice begins to brown. Then take a vine leaf in your left hand and wrong side upward and put a little of this prepared rice into it. Put some of the coarse vine leaves at the bottom of the paper bag and arrange each little ball beside its neighbor, packing them rather tightly. When this is done, put in sufficient water just to cover the dolmas, add a little oil, seal the bag and bake till the rice is soft and the water is all absorbed. This is a very delicate and characteristic dish, but will be a failure if the vine leaves are not tender or the oil is rancid. Serve with lemon.

CHAPTER XVIII.

WARM BREADS, BISCUITS, MUFFINS, ETC.

Baking Powder Bread.—SIFT together, five times over, four quarts of flour, six rounded teaspoonfuls baking powder and four level teaspoonfuls salt. Have the oven quite hot. Add to the sifted flour enough milk and water in nearly equal proportions, to make a moist, not wet, dough, stiff enough to handle, then divide into four portions, mould lightly into shape and put into brick shaped pans. Brush over the tops with milk, put into bags and bake an hour.

Bannocks.—Sift together one pint of corn meal, one tablespoonful of sugar and a teaspoonful of salt. Pour over the mixture enough milk or milk and water to moisten. Let stand until cool, then add three well-beaten eggs, spread half an inch thick in well-greased bag. Seal and bake in hot oven. Cut into squares, split and serve hot and well-buttered.

Baking Powder Biscuits.—Sift together three times over one quart of flour, two rounded teaspoonfuls baking powder, and a teaspoonful of salt. Rub in with the tips of the fingers one rounding tablespoonful vegetable shortening or butter, and when the flour feels mealy, add slowly a cup and a half of milk or milk and water mixed. Mix lightly with little handling, turn out on board, roll into a sheet half an inch in thickness, stamp out with small round cutter and lay in greased bag. Brush the top of each biscuit with milk. Seal and bake twenty minutes in a very hot oven.

Egg Biscuits.—To make these delicious biscuits, beat one egg until light, then mix with it two-thirds of a cupful of milk. Add to one pint of flour a heaping teaspoonful baking powder and one-half teaspoonful salt, and sift. Blend with the mixture one tablespoonful of butter and two tablespoonfuls of sugar. Add the egg mixture, make into a dough and knead lightly. Roll into a sheet a quarter of an inch thick, stamp out with a round cutter, brush over the top of each biscuit with cream, prick with a fork, bag, and bake in a hot oven.

Maple Biscuits.—Make a very rich baking powder biscuit dough and roll out to half the thickness of biscuits, cut out with a small cutter, sprinkle grated maple sugar over the tops of half of them, moisten the under sides of the others and lay them on top of the sugared ones, pressing them on well. Lay close together in a bag, brush over with milk or melted butter, seal and bake in a quick oven.

Nut Biscuits.—Sift together two cupfuls flour, one-half teaspoonful of salt, and a teaspoonful and a half of baking powder.

Rub in one heaping tablespoonful of butter or vegetable shortening, and add one cupful of nuts, pecans, hickory or English walnuts chopped and a tablespoonful of sugar. Mix to a soft dough with milk or milk and water, mould with the hands into small balls, place in a greased bag, brush each biscuit over with milk or melted butter, put a pinch of chopped nuts on each, seal and bake in a hot oven.

Raisin Biscuits.—These are excellent for home luncheon or the children's school or picnic lunch. Sift together one quart of flour, a half teaspoonful of salt and two heaping teaspoonfuls of baking powder. Work into the sifted flour a cupful of shortening, then add a cupful each seedless raisins and milk. Mix well and roll out on the molding board. Cut in small round biscuits, bag, and bake in a quick oven.

Hot Cross Buns.—Sift together one quart of pastry flour, three teaspoonfuls of baking powder and a teaspoonful of salt. Rub into the flour a piece of butter the size of an egg. Mix together a cupful each of milk and water and add one cupful of sugar. Stir into the flour, add two beaten eggs, and mix soft. Cut into small biscuits, make the cross on the top of each, bag, and bake in a very hot oven. Sift powdered sugar over them as soon as taken from the bag. A half cupful chopped raisins or currants may be added to the dough if desired.

Warmed Over Breads.—It is a trick worth knowing that cold biscuit, rolls, gems and the like can be brushed over with water, put in a greased paper bag, sealed and set in the oven for eight minutes to emerge as fresh as though just newly baked.

CHAPTER XIX.

CAKES.

CAKES baked in paper bags will be as brown as if baked without the bag and will retain their moisture infinitely better; therefore plain loaf cakes and all fruit cakes are greatly improved by the paper bag cooking. While drop cakes, oatmeal cookies and the like can be baked directly on the bottom of the bag, better results as far as form is concerned, will come from using very thin tin moulds or baking sheets or paper souffle cases. Before putting a cake in the oven, particularly if it be a fruit cake, it will be found advisable to set on the bottom of the oven, a shallow pan with a little water in it. Put in the bag, close the oven door and leave ten minutes with the gas on, then reduce the heat at least one-half. Bag cooking prevents cake crusting over and thereby permits it to rise to its full height. It also saves from burning. Midway in the baking the position of cakes can be changed, those on the grid itself set low on the broiler and vice versa so all will cook evenly. To test whether the cake is done or no, make a hole in the bag top and thrust in a clean straw or thin knife blade. If it comes out dry with no stickiness, the cake is done.

Cheese Cakes.—These are a modern adaptation of the old "flawns," a favorite Eastertide cake. As formerly made, there was a tedious separation of curds and whey; but the housewife of today eliminates that by taking a Neufchatel or cream cheese as the foundation. This is crumbled fine and added to the other ingredients, allowing to each Neufchatel cheese, one small cupful of sugar, the grated rind and half the juice of one lemon, a half cupful each sifted cracker crumbs and currants, one tablespoonful melted butter, half a nutmeg grated, half a cupful of cream or rich milk, a saltspoonful of salt and four eggs. Crumble the cheese and crackers together, beat the eggs and add, together with sugar, salt and spices. Next add the butter and cream and lastly the currants, lemon juice and rind. Mix thoroughly and fill patty tins lined with puff paste. Ornament the top with currants and slender strips of citron, put in buttered bag. Seal and bake in a quick oven.

Cinnamon Cake.—Cream one-quarter cup of butter and one cup of sugar, add one-half cup of milk, one well beaten egg, one and three-quarters cups of flour sifted twice with three even teaspoons of baking powder, and pour in a shallow pan to make a sheet rather than a loaf. Just before setting the cake into the oven sprinkle cinnamon and granulated sugar over the top. Put into a bag. Seal and bake twenty minutes. Serve fresh and cut in squares.

English Fairy Cakes.—Sift together six ounces of flour and a half teaspoonful of baking powder. Grate a lemon rind and add to the sifted flour together with three ounces chopped candied cherries. Beat to a cream four ounces of butter and four of sugar, then add three eggs one at a time, beating thoroughly. Add the flour and cherry mixture and stir lightly. Have ready some buttered patty-tins, half fill with the batter, bag, and bake in a moderate oven twenty minutes.

Fruit Cookies.—One cupful and one-half of sugar, either white or brown, one cupful of butter and lard or vegetable shortening, (half and half is good) three tablespoonfuls of molasses, the same amount of hot water, three eggs, one cupful of raisins, one teaspoonful each of soda (dissolved in hot water), ginger and cinnamon, a light sprinkling of cloves, and flour to make very stiff. Half a cupful or more of chopped nut meats makes a nice addition, but is not necessary.

Cream the sugar and shortening, as for cake, then add eggs well beaten, molasses and water, spices and soda, then flour, and lastly fruit. When the batter will take up no more flour, lift it up by teaspoonfuls, pat it flat and in shape in the baking pan, which must be well-buttered, put in bag, and bake in fairly hot oven, being careful not to scorch.

This will be found much easier than rolling the dough on a board, and will make about forty cookies.

Mrs. Godfrey's Soft Gingerbread.—In a symposium on gingerbreads held one Summer afternoon at Sunapee Inn, New Hampshire, this was given as an example of a most delicate inexpensive cake. Add to one cupful molasses, one cupful softened butter or lard, filling up the cup in which it is measured with boiling water. Add two even teaspoonfuls soda, a small teaspoonful of ginger, a pinch of salt, one beaten egg, and two heaping cupfuls sifted flour. Beat lightly (not too much lest it make the ginger bread light colored), put in bag and bake in a moderate oven.

Good Friday Cake.—This is a simple tea cake, not very sweet, and is served hot or cold as preferred. To make it, beat to a cream a scant cupful of butter and a quarter cupful of sugar. Add a teaspoonful of the grated yellow rind of lemon, a half teaspoonful of lemon juice, a pound of flour and enough water to make a stiff paste. Divide the dough into two equal parts and roll into large, round cakes about the size of an ordinary pie tin. Mark the edges with a "jigger" into some fancy design, or simply pinch with the fingers. Cut each cake into quarters, brush over with the white of an egg, lay a strip of candied lemon peel on each, sprinkle with granulated sugar put in bag, and bake.

German Honey Cakes.—These are fine for luncheon or the kaffee klatch. Put into a saucepan two cupfuls strained honey and one cupful sugar. Warm, add a cupful of butter and a half tablespoonful soda dissolved in a little warm water. Add a half cupful caraway seed and flour to roll. Roll into a rather thick sheet, mark into squares, put in bag, and bake. When done cut in small cakes.

Pecan Kisses.—Into the whites of six eggs put fourteen little more than level tablespoonfuls white sugar and beat long and thoroughly until stiff enough to stand alone. Have ready a small cup pecan kernels having them in as perfect halves as possible. Beat in lightly, drop in greased baking sheet, put in bag. Seal and bake in a moderate oven.

Mrs. Kelder's Loaf Cake.—Beat to a cream one and one-half cupfuls sugar and one-half cupful of butter. Add the yolks of three eggs beaten until light and thin. Add two and one-half cupfuls flour measured after sifting with two heaping teaspoonfuls of baking powder. Lastly fold in the stiffly whipped whites of three eggs and flavor to taste. Put in light tin, set in paper bag. Seal and bake thirty-five minutes.

Hickory Nut Macaroons.—To one whole egg beaten light, add one cup sugar and beat well. Add two tablespoonfuls flour and one cup nut meats and lastly fold in the stiffly whipped whites of three eggs. Drop by spoonfuls into a well-greased bag and bake in a moderate oven ten or twelve minutes.

Walnut Macaroons.—One and one-half cupfuls of sugar, one-third cup of butter, three eggs, three cups of flour, one teaspoonful of soda, dissolved in water, one teaspoonful of cloves, one teaspoonful of cinnamon, one cup of English walnut meats, one cup of chopped dates. Do not roll the mixture as in ordinary cookies, but drop into a greased bag with a spoon. Seal and bake slowly for thirty minutes.

Maple Sugar Cake.—Add to one cup maple syrup one beaten egg, a pinch of salt, one cup of thick, sour cream, into which has been stirred a teaspoonful (scant) of soda, a teaspoonful of ginger and flour to make a thin batter. Bake in a bag and cut in squares.

Molasses Coffee Cake.—Then right here let me give you a recipe for a fruit cake or gingerbread with fruit as you may elect to call it. Cream together one cupful of sugar and three-fourths cup of butter. Add one cupful black molasses, one cupful strong coffee with a teaspoonful of soda dissolved in it, four beaten eggs, one teaspoonful each cinnamon and nutmeg, three-fourths teaspoonful cloves, one half pound shredded citron and three cupfuls sifted flour. Do not beat longer than necessary. Put in tin, then in bag, and bake in a slow oven.

Nut Cake.—To make a light, delicious cake, cream together one cup of sugar and five tablespoons of melted butter. Into this beat two well beaten eggs, a pinch of salt and a cup of milk. Stir into this two heaping cupfuls of flour, sifted with two heaping teaspoonfuls of baking powder. After this is well beaten, stir in three-quarters of a cup of chopped walnuts. Bake in square cake tin in bag. Ice when cold with plain pulverized sugar icing. Cut in squares, placing a piece of walnut meat on each square.

Oatmeal Cakes.—Beat to a cream three-fourths cupful vegetable shortening or butter and a cupful and a half of brown sugar. Dissolve one teaspoonful of soda in one cupful of boiling water and add to butter and sugar mixture. Mix together two cupfuls of dry oatmeal, two cupfuls of flour and a half teaspoonful of salt and add to the other ingredients. Flavor to taste. Lastly add two well beaten eggs and drop from spoon into greased bag or flat tin and place in bag. Seal and bake in moderate oven about fifteen minutes.

German Peach Cake.—Make a rich baking powder biscuit dough and roll out in sheets to fit a long biscuit pan. It should not be more than a half-inch thick. Brush the top with butter and cover with slices of peach arranged in symmetrical overlapping rows, or half peaches with the rounded side up. Sprinkle generously with sugar, cover with another tin to prevent the fruit from becoming mushy or hardened, put in bag and bake about half an hour in a hot oven. This is a good substitute for peach pie.

Pork Cake.—This is an old New England dish that has been relegated to the background these many years, but is lately coming to the fore. A gray haired New York physician, dining at my house the other night, declared that his old Connecticut aunt's pork cake was one of the dearest remembered gustatorial delights of his boyhood.

To make it chop one pound of fat pork fine. Pour over it a pint of boiling water, then stir in three cupfuls brown sugar, one pound of seeded raisins, eight cupfuls of flour and two rounding teaspoonfuls of soda dissolved in a little water. Add a teaspoonful of cinnamon, a half teaspoonful cloves and nutmeg, mix thoroughly and bake in a slow oven like fruit cake. If preferred, two beaten eggs may be added in which case less flour will be required.

Potato Chocolate Cake.—To two cupfuls of sugar and two-thirds cup butter beaten to a cream, add yolks of four eggs beaten until lemon colored and light and a half cupful of sweet milk. Next add a teaspoonful of soda dissolved in two tablespoonfuls of hot water, one cup mashed potato, two cups of flour, and four squares of chocolate melted, one cup chopped walnuts, a teaspoonful of vanilla. Lastly fold in the stiffly beaten whites of four eggs. This may be baked either in a large loaf or in layers in a paper bag.

Potato Caramel Cake.—Beat to a cream two-thirds cup of butter and two cups of sugar, add the yolks of four eggs beaten until light and mix with a half cup of sweet milk and one cup mashed potato. Add two squares of bitter chocolate melted, one-half teaspoonful nutmeg, and two cups flour sifted with two teaspoonfuls baking powder. Fold in whites of four eggs beaten stiff, a cupful of nut meats, preferably English walnuts, chopped. Bake slowly for about an hour in a gingerbread tin in paper bag, making the cake an inch and a half or two inches thick; or else in layer tins together with white icing. This will make four layers.

Auburn Pound Cake.—Beat to a cream three-fourths pounds of butter and one pound fine granulated sugar. Add the yolks of nine eggs beaten light and one pound flour measured after sifting and then sifted again with a teaspoonful and a half of baking powder. Fold in the stiffly whipped whites and flavor with vanilla, almond or the grated rind and juice of a lemon or a wine glass of sherry. Pour into well-buttered thin tin mould and seal in bags. Bake an hour and a quarter or an hour and a half in a moderate oven.

Raisin Nut Cakes.—For raisin nut cakes for afternoon tea, beat six eggs lightly, beating the whites and with an even teaspoon of soda, one teaspoon of sugar creamed with a cupful of butter, a cupful and a half of milk and three cupfuls and a half of flour. Add a cupful of chopped walnuts, two pounds of chopped raisins, a wineglass of brandy, two teaspoonfuls of baking powder and spice to taste. Make into small cakes, put on tin in bag and bake in a moderate oven.

Sour Cream Cake.—Beat together one cup of powdered sugar and one cup of sour cream, add two eggs beaten light, one and one-half cups of flour sifted twice with an even teaspoon of soda twice, one teaspoon of vanilla and one cup of seeded and cut raisins rolled lightly in flour. Beat to make the batter creamy and bake at once in a rather shallow pan sealed in a paper bag.

CHAPTER XX.

FRUITS.

Baked Apples.—WASH, but do not peel; cut out specks and bruises, core, fill the bottom of the core-space with a bit of butter, over which pile sugar and add a dusting of cinnamon. A clove stuck in the side may take the place of the cinnamon. Seal inside a well-greased bag and bake eighteen to twenty minutes in a fairly hot oven. Serve hot with sugar and cream or a hard sauce.

Baked Apple Dumplings.—Make a regular shortcake crust, using one pint of flour, two teaspoonfuls baking powder and a saltspoonful of salt, sifted together three times, one-quarter cup butter rubbed in with the tips of the fingers, and one egg beaten and mixed with three-quarters cup milk. Roll out and cut in five-inch squares. Have ready three large apples, peeled, cored and halved and lay each piece on a square of the paste. Fold the pastry over each apple like a blanket, lapping the four corners at the top and pressing them down firmly. Turn the dumplings upside down in a well-buttered bag, dot with bits of butter and sprinkle with sugar. Set the bag in a quick oven and bake to a russet brown. This will take about half an hour. Serve with any sweet sauce, or rich, sweet cream.

Cold Baked Apples With Rum.—Peel, core and bake the apples in a buttered bag, with a teaspoonful of sugar to each apple. Put in the serving dish, and while still very hot pour over each a dessertspoonful of rum. Let cool and serve with cake or crisped water biscuit.

Cinnamon Apples.—Peel, core and quarter six good cooking apples, preferably greenings. Melt a tablespoonful of butter in a warm bowl and stir the apples in it until coated with the butter. Mix a teaspoonful of ground cinnamon with a half cup of granulated sugar, and stir into the apples. Have a paper bag thoroughly buttered and put the apples in it. Rinse out the bowl with a cup of hot water, add it to the apples, seal carefully, place on a broiler which rests on a pie plate and bake in a hot oven fifteen minutes. Half a pint of whipped cream over the apples when served is an addition, but they are delicious, cooked in this way, without it.

Apples Stuffed With Figs.—Steam tender as many figs as you desire, chop into dice and roll each piece in powdered sugar seasoned with cinnamon. Core large, tart apples and fill the cavities with the figs. Bag and bake in a hot oven, adding a little hot water. When tender, remove carefully to the serving dish and pour over them a syrup made by boiling a half cup of sugar with an equal quantity of water. Flavor to taste and pour over the apples. Serve cold with whipped or plain cream.

Baked Apples and Nuts.—For a half dozen large apples a good three-fourths cup of nut meats, butternuts, black walnuts or hickory nuts—will be required. Chop the meats fine and add a half cup of sugar. Core the apples and fill the centres with the nuts and sugar. Put in a rather deep pan, with a cupful of boiling water added, bag and bake. When tender remove carefully, place in a pretty dish, pour the juice over the apples, and crown with whipped cream or a meringue made from the whites of two eggs.

Raisin Apples.—A simple dessert enjoyed by the children consists of apples, cored and each cavity filled with sugar, nutmeg, a bit of butter and two or three raisins. Add one cupful of hot water, put in bag and bake in a slow oven. This may be varied occasionally by placing a meringue on the top of each apple when done, and cooking in a slow oven for seven minutes longer. Serve cold.

Baked Apple Sauce.—Peel and core firm apples of good flavor. Stick three cloves in each and put bits of mace and cinnamon in the core spaces. Put them in a well-buttered bag with two heaping cupfuls of sugar and a half cupful of water. Cook thirty minutes. Have the oven very hot at first, but slack heat after seven minutes. Lemon juice instead of water makes a richer flavored sauce. In that case add a half cupful more sugar at the outset.

Baked Bananas.—Peel and remove coarse threads, cut the pulp in halves lengthwise, dust with sugar and sprinkle with lemon juice, put in buttered bag and bake fifteen minutes, or roll the bananas in hot marmalade, then bake.

Stuffed Dates.—Select large, fine fruit, wash quickly and remove the pit. Put into the cavity a bit of crystallized ginger or citron, a nut or little candied peel, roll in confectioner's sugar and lay in lightly buttered bag left open at one end. Put in coolish oven to harden.

Baked Gooseberries.—Put into a greased bag a pint of "topped and tailed" gooseberries, add a cupful each sugar and water, seal and cook twenty minutes.

Baked Peaches.—Pour boiling water over the fruit, then rub off the skins and place in buttered bag without removing the pits. Add a teaspoonful of water for each peach, seal and bake about twenty minutes in a hot oven. When done, sweeten to taste and set aside to chill before using. Serve with sweet cream.

Baked Pears.—Select ripe, fine-flavored fruit, snip out the blossom end and stick in a clove. If the skin is thin, do not peel, but if tough, remove, put in buttered bag with a little water, seal and cook from fifteen to thirty minutes according to the quality of the fruit.

Baked Plums.—Put in buttered bag with a little water and cook twenty or twenty-five minutes. Sweeten to taste when done.

Baked Quinces.—Wash, core and peel, fill the centers with sugar and put in greased bag with two tablespoonfuls of water allowed for each quince. Seal and bake slowly for an hour, until the quince is tender but not mushy. Serve with the quince syrup and a spoonful of whipped cream on top of each quince.

Baked Raisins.—Remove stems, clean well, put in a colander and wash thoroughly. Put in buttered bag with a cupful of water for each cupful of raisins. Seal and cook slowly for half an hour. A mixture of dried apricots, prunes and cherries is nice with the raisins, but these fruits need long soaking in cold water before adding to the raisins and cooking.

Chestnut Patties.—Beat together, until smooth, one egg and one cupful of pulverized sugar. Add one cupful of chestnut meats that have been put through a nut grinder, five tablespoonfuls of flour and one teaspoonful of baking powder. Beat lightly, then drop by spoonfuls on buttered tins. Dust with pulverized sugar and cinnamon. Put in bag and bake in a quick oven.

CHAPTER XXI.

PASTRY.

USE tin or agate pie plates for paper bag cookery. Line with a delicate crust, and prick the bottom with a fork. Turn in whatever filling you elect to have, and put on top crust or the latticed bars. Cut a cross in the center of a solid crust and turn back the points or prick with a fork. Any pie can be baked in a paper bag with advantage. Cook two pies at once, shifting midway in the cooking from the upper to the lower shelves and vice versa. Have the oven hot when the pies go in, but reduce the heat as soon as the bag corners turn brown. Average pies require about half an hour for the baking.

Plain Pie Crust.—For each pie allow a heaping cupful of pastry flour and sift into a cold bowl with a half teaspoonful of salt and a saltspoonful of baking powder. Have ready a quarter cupful of butter that has been washed in cold water, then chilled on the ice. Work into the sifted flour a quarter cupful of lard or vegetable shortening, using the tips of the fingers or a case knife. As soon as the flour begins to feel like coarse meal, moisten to a dough with cold water. Add a little at a time, handling the crust as lightly as possible. It will take about a quarter of a cupful of water to a heaping cupful of flour. Toss on a smooth board, dredged lightly with flour, pat and roll a quarter of an inch in thickness, keeping the sheet of paste a little wider than it is long. Now place the chilled butter on the center of the lower half of the paste and cover by folding the upper part of the sheet over it. Press the edges together so as to inclose as much air as possible. Fold the right side of the paste over the inclosed butter and the left side under. Turn the paste half way around, pat into shape and roll out lightly having the sheet of paste longer than it is wide, and lifting often to prevent its sticking to the board. Dredge slightly with flour when necessary. Fold again so as to make three layers, divide in halves, pat and roll out the one intended for the lower crust having it a little larger than the pie plate, to allow for shrinkage. Fold back the rolled out crust and readjust in the pie tin letting it come well up over the edge, then pressing back. Turn in the filling then roll out the upper crust. When this reaches the required size, fold over and perforate the center, piercing with a fork or using a knife to make any pattern desired, and place in position over the pie.

Apple Pie.—Peel and slice thin, tart, well flavored apples. Put in crust, sprinkle with sugar, dust with cinnamon or nutmeg, cover with latticed or full crust, put in bag, and bake half an hour in a steady oven.

A New Apple Pie.—Peel and core about eight or ten apples or as many as are wanted. Make a rich pastry dough and cut in strips about two inches wide. Wind a strip around each apple, but do not cover it. Fill the center of each apple with butter, sugar and water. Sprinkle with nutmeg, put in bag, then in the oven and bake. Serve with or without cream.

Deep Apple Pie With Cream Cheese.—Bake a nice apple pie about three-quarters of an hour before dinner. Have a small cream cheese pressed through a ricer and mixed with a cup of whipped cream and a little salt. Press through a pastry tube or tin funnel on top of the pie in a pattern, and serve warm for dessert. The cheese and cream combination may also be used on a two crust apple pie.

Cranberry Pie.—Line a rather deep pie plate with a plain crust. Put on a border of richer paste, fill with cranberries cooked according to directions for stewed cranberries, and put strips of crust over the top, making squares or diamonds as preferred. Put in bag and bake.

Cranberry and Raisin Pie.—Allow to each pie a cup and a half cranberries and a half cup of raisins. The latter should be seeded and the berries washed and cut in two. Mix with them a cup of sugar, a tablespoon of flour, and a teaspoonful of butter. Fill a pie plate lined with crust, heaping up slightly in the middle. Cover with an upper crust, bag, and bake in a hot oven.

Lemon Pie.—Beat the yolks of three eggs lightly, add one cup of sugar slowly and then the juice and grated yellow rind of one lemon. Beat hard and stir in two even tablespoons of flour made smooth in one cup of milk. Turn into a paste lined plate and bake about half an hour in a paper bag. Cool partly and cover with the whites of three eggs beaten stiff with six even tablespoons of powdered sugar. Pile roughly and set in a very cool oven to become firm.

Mince Pie.—A simple rule for making mince meat by measure, calls for a pint bowl of well cooked beef chopped to the finest mince and measured after chopping, two bowls of tart apples chopped into coarse bits and a half bowl chopped suet. Add to this a pound of seeded raisins, also chopped, a pound of currants, a quarter of a pound of citron cut in thin slices, a tablespoonful each of powdered cinnamon, cloves and nutmeg. Use enough sweet cider to make moist, then add a bowl of sugar and an even teaspoonful salt. Scald well and put away in a stone jar. When you make the pies add a few whole raisins, chopped nut meats or any jelly you have on hand.

When mince pie is to be reheated for dinner and served hot, grated cheese may be sprinkled over the top just before setting it in the oven to heat.

Mock Mince Pie.—To four quarts green tomatoes, chopped fine, allow three pounds brown sugar, the juice of two lemons and their yellow rind, grated, a tablespoonful each cinnamon, allspice and salt, half a teaspoonful cloves and a tablespoonful of grated nutmeg. Put into a porcelain lined kettle and simmer gently until reduced one half in bulk. Now add two pounds and one-half seeded raisins, or part raisins and part currants or chopped prunes and a cup of boiled cider. Then cook an hour or two longer until thick. Bake as any mince pie.

Pecan Pie With One Crust.—One cup of sugar, three eggs, one cup of sweet cream, one cup of pecans well mashed. Beat very light, pour into two pie pans that are lined with good rich paste, put in bag and bake.

Real Old Fashioned Pumpkin Pie.—If you are fortunate enough to get a genuine old fashioned field pumpkin, you may be thankful. If forbidden that privilege, the canned pumpkin or the dried pumpkin flour, or again a Hubbard squash or a big yellow one, may be so manipulated as to deceive even a connoisseur on pumpkin pies, into thinking he has the very kind that "Mother used to make," and giving thanks accordingly. If the field pumpkin is yours, wash, cut up without peeling, scrape out all the wooly fiber, then put over the fire on the back of the stove. Add just a little water to keep it from sticking on the bottom, cover closely and steam gently for six or eight hours. At the end of this time the pumpkin pulp should be thoroughly cooked in its own juices. Take up, cool a little, then pull off the skin with a sharp knife. Press through a sieve and let it stand overnight in a press so as to remove the superfluous liquid, which should be saved to use in making Boston brown bread. When ready to bake, measure the pulp and to every five cupfuls allow one teaspoonful of salt, half a grated nutmeg, a tablespoonful of mace, two teaspoonfuls of ginger and a large cupful of sugar. Beat four eggs and stir into the pumpkin pulp, together with four cupfuls of sweet milk and a half cupful cream. Beat well and taste to see if it is sweet enough. Turn into plates lined with good pastry, bag, and bake three-quarters of an hour until a golden brown and firm in the center. Serve with good American cheese. Some old-fashioned cooks like their pumpkin pies flavored with a little rose water.

In making pies of the canned pumpkin, observe the same proportions. If the pumpkin flour is used, spread on a tin and brown before adding the milk.

The English fashion of baking pumpkin as well as mince pies in individual shells, is preferred by many who do not feel the compelling force of tradition. A new wrinkle for the woman who holds to her pumpkin pie for Thanksgiving, but wishes to present it in very modern guise is to serve it with cottage cheese balls and strained honey. The combination of flavors is certainly a most happy one. The cheese balls are piled in a pretty dish and the honey served from a glass bowl.

Individual English Apple Tart.—Peel and core tart apples, put into a large saucepan, cover with boiling water, stew gently until the apples are tender but unbroken. Sweeten to taste. Line the edges of a deep pie tin with crust, then fill the center of the dish with apples, dropping into the center of each a spoonful of orange marmalade. Cover the top of the dish with strips of pastry arranged lattice fashion, bag, and bake quickly until brown. Serve hot.

Colonial Pumpkin Tartlets.—To one quart of cooked and sifted pumpkin add one tablespoonful each of butter and flour, six well beaten eggs, a cupful of sugar, a quarter teaspoonful each of mace and nutmeg, four teaspoonfuls of ginger and one gill of milk. Bake in patty-pans lined with rich flaky crust, set in paper bag. Remove from pans before serving. A touch of novelty is given by topping each tartlet with a generous portion of maple syrup or strained honey.

TURNOVERS.

Apple and Cheese Turnovers.—Make a crust, using six heaping tablespoonfuls of flour, three tablespoonfuls lard and butter, half and half, a saltspoonful of salt and just enough water to roll out. Mark out into squares of about four inches. Have ready some nice tart apples sliced fine, and also cheese sliced very thin. Fill each one with apples, sprinkle sugar and cinnamon over the apple, put a tiny piece of butter on top, then turn up the edges of the crust, overlapping the upper side about two inches. Place in a buttered bag, and having wet the edges of the crust with milk, bake to a nice brown. Remove from the oven, raise up the upper crust, put in the cheese, re-cover, turn a tin over the turnovers and stand in the oven again for ten minutes, leaving the oven door open. This softens the cheese. Eat while warm. Caraway seeds may be used in place of cinnamon if desired. The turnovers may be eaten plain with cream or with a liquid sauce as preferred.

Apricot or Plum Jam Turnovers.—Make a good crust and roll out twice. Mark a square and spread thickly with jam. Fold over two sides first and pinch together, then fold over the other two sides in the same way. Brush over with milk and sprinkle with brown sugar. Put into well-greased bag and bake thirty minutes.

Mince Turnovers.—Make the original round of paste about four inches across. Put a tablespoonful of mince meat upon it, fold over very neatly and pinch the edges together. Flatten and cook inside a buttered bag.

CHAPTER XXI.

SHORT CAKES

Banana Short Cake.—BEAT to a cream one-half cupful butter and one of sugar. Add two well-beaten eggs, a pinch of salt and a teaspoonful of baking powder sifted with a pint of flour. Flavor with vanilla. Mix lightly and roll out into a sheet about half an inch thick. Cut into rounds about four inches in diameter, and having brushed each one over with melted butter, pile on top of each other and put in buttered bag. Bake twelve minutes, separate, and spread between the layers a thick filling of sliced bananas flavored with lemon juice and sweetened to taste. Serve with Foamy Sauce.

Peach Short Cake.—Use for this either fresh peaches or canned and make in one large short cake or individual ones which are really nicer in paper bag cookery. For the latter sift together a pint and a half of flour, two tablespoonfuls of salt. Rub in with the tips of the fingers two tablespoonfuls of butter, then add one beaten egg and milk to make a soft dough. Cut out like biscuit, bag and bake in a quick oven. When baked, split in two, spread lightly with butter and fill with the sweetened peaches and whipped cream, a layer of peaches first and cream on top. Cover the little short cakes in the same way, piling up the whipped cream on top.

Rhubarb Short Cake.—Stew rhubarb and sweeten to taste. Make a short cake batter, using one-quarter cupful of butter and a half cupful sugar creamed together, one egg well beaten, one quarter cupful sweet milk and one cupful of flour sifted with one teaspoonful of baking powder. Make in two large layers or individual ones, and bake in paper bag. When done, spread with the rhubarb filling and serve with whipped cream or a cream sauce.

Old Fashioned Strawberry Short Cake.—The real old-fashioned strawberry short cake may be made with sour cream or rich sour milk and soda, or sweet milk and baking powder. Sometimes an egg is added and a tablespoonful of sugar, but it is a far cry from the French strawberry short cake of hotels and restaurants which is really a cake, either sponge or layer, with whole berries between the layers and thick whipped cream or a meringue on top. To make the genuine old-fashioned sour milk biscuit short cake, which is really more tender than that made with sweet milk, put four cups sifted pastry flour in a mixing bowl with a half teaspoonful of salt and mix well. Add three tablespoonfuls of butter and chop fine, using a silver knife. Dissolve a level teaspoonful of soda in a little hot water and stir into a large cupful of sour cream or rich sour milk. When it stops "purring" add a tablespoonful of sugar and one well beaten egg to the milk and turn into the sifted flour. Mix well together with a spatula or flexible knife, handling as little as possible, then turn out on to a floured board. The dough should be soft enough to roll easily. Divide and roll lightly and quickly into two thin sheets. These may be baked separately in well-greased round tins in a paper bag or laid one on top of the other with a thin coating of butter between and baked in one bag. Bake in a very hot oven. When done, separate. Have ready a quart of ripe berries washed, crushed and sugared. This should have been done before beginning the dough, so that the sugar will have time to draw out the rich juice of the berries. Cover the lower half of the short cake with a thick layer of these berries, place the second cake on top and cover with the rest of the crushed and sweetened berries or large whole ones dusted with powdered sugar. Serve with thick cream or a crushed berry sauce.

PUDDINGS.

Almond Pudding.—Blanche one pound of almonds and grind to a smooth paste with two teaspoonfuls of rose water. Add a wine glass of wine and a half cupful of cream thickened with a large spoonful of bread crumbs. Add a half pound of sugar, seven well beaten eggs and a half teaspoonful of grated nutmeg. Put in a thin walled pudding dish, set in bag, seal and bake half an hour.

Apple and Fig Pudding.—Select large tart baking apples, wash and core. Stuff each apple with a fig rolled small as possible or chopped, as preferred. Put in buttered bag and bake slowly until tender, but not broken. Place in a glass dish and cover with a thick boiled custard. Decorate each apple with a candied or Maraschino cherry and serve with sweet wafers.

Banana Pudding.—Beat the yolks of three eggs and whites of two. Add a cupful of sugar, a scant half cupful softened butter, a cupful stale cake crumbs and a cupful of milk. Beat all together well, then add three bananas sliced thin, and the juice of a half lemon. Put into a basin then in a well-buttered bag, seal and bake half an hour, take out, cover with a meringue made from the whipped white of the egg that was left over and a tablespoonful of sugar with a little lemon juice to flavor. Strew a little candied peel over the meringue and set in the oven, which should be quite cool for the meringue to rise slowly and stiffen. Serve with lemon sauce.

Farmer's Plum Pudding.—Put into a basin two cupfuls of flour sifted with two level teaspoonfuls baking powder, a pinch of salt and a level teaspoonful ginger and cinnamon. Add one-half cupful sugar, one cupful chopped suet, one-half cupful each candied peel and currants and raisins. Make to batter consistency with one-half cupful each molasses and milk and one beaten egg. Put in small buttered molds, set in paper bag, pour in enough cold water to come three parts up the sides, seal and bake two hours, reducing the heat of the oven after the first ten minutes. Serve with hard or foamy sauce.

Peach Betty.—Sprinkle a layer of crumbs in a buttered baking dish and over this a layer of peach quarters. Sprinkle with sugar, then repeat a layer of crumbs and peaches and sugar until the dish is filled, having the crumbs on top. Put in buttered bag and bake thirty-five minutes in a moderate oven, and serve with sweetened cream. To prepare the buttered crumbs melt a little butter and pour over the crumbs.

Peach Cobbler.—For this the richest and ripest peaches are none too good. Some variety of the yellow peach is usually chosen because of its superior richness. For its baking a pudding dish at least three and a half inches deep is chosen. This is lined with a rich crust, a square of the dough being taken from the bottom. Now peel enough ripe and luscious peaches to fill the dish, tearing them apart but leaving the pits in to impart their superior flavor. Sweeten abundantly, add about two tablespoonfuls water, and a tablespoonful of butter cut in bits. Cover with a layer of puff paste, sealing it down carefully on the sides to the border, so as to lose none of the juices. Bag and bake in a quick oven for forty-five minutes. When nearly done, draw to the edge of the oven, open the top of the bag, dust with powdered sugar and set back a few moments longer for the crust to glaze. This is perfection, whether eaten hot or cold, serving it alone, with cream or with a hard sauce as preferred.

Peach Roly Poly.—Make a sweet biscuit dough. Roll out thin and spread with a layer of sliced or chopped peaches and roll the dough over as for jelly roll. Put in buttered bag and bake in a moderate oven.

Plum Roly Poly.—Wash and stew any ripe sound plums and remove the pits. If very juicy, drain away the most of the juice. Sweeten to taste. Make a good biscuit dough or puff paste as preferred, roll out in long strips, sprinkle sugar on the upper side, then spread thinly with the stewed plums, roll up and pinch the ends tight. Put in buttered bag and cook thirty minutes. Serve with a sauce made from the extra juice sweetened and slightly thickened with a little cornstarch.

Rye Bread Pudding.—Toast stale rye bread to a golden brown, then roll into fine crumbs. Brush small custard cups or a mould with melted butter, sprinkle over a few currants, raisins, prunes (cut fine) or figs, then fill with crumbs. Beat three eggs without separating until light, add three tablespoonfuls of sugar, a pint of milk (with vanilla or nutmeg to flavor) and pour carefully over the bread crumbs. Let them stand ten minutes, until the mixture has soaked into the crumbs; then set in a paper bag in a pan of cold water and cook like a custard in the oven. It will take about half an hour. Test by slipping the blade of the knife down the side of the bag. If it comes up clear, the pudding is sufficiently baked. Serve hot with lemon or egg sauce or fruit syrup.

Tapioca Apple Pudding.—Soak one cupful tapioca in three pints cold water over night. In the morning put on to boil and cook twenty or thirty minutes, until it looks clear. Add a quart and a half peeled and quartered apples, one cup of sugar, a teaspoonful salt, and lemon juice or extract to flavor. Turn into a buttered dish, put in bag and bake an hour in a moderate oven. When cold serve with cream and sugar.

A White Plum Pudding.—Beat to a cream a half cup of sugar and three-quarters cup of butter. Add four eggs well beaten, a saltspoonful of salt, two cups milk, a quart of flour mixed with one-half cup shredded citron, one-half cup currants, a teaspoonful grated nutmeg and a teaspoonful vanilla. Just before turning into the mould stir in two even tablespoonfuls pure baking powder. Put in bag, surround with water, steam two hours and serve with any good sauce.

PUDDING SAUCES.

Caramel Sauce.—Put one-half cupful of sugar over the fire in a clean, smooth saucepan and stir until it becomes a light brown color. Pour in a half cupful of boiling water, simmer ten minutes, add a tablespoonful of butter and serve with pudding or fritters.

Cornstarch Pudding Sauce.—Beat together one tablespoonful cornstarch, two tablespoonfuls of butter and a half cupful of brown sugar. Set on the stove until heated, then turn in hot water a little at a time and cook until consistency required. Add four tablespoonfuls of grape or apple jelly with spices or other flavoring to taste, and serve hot.

Cream Sauce.—Mix together two tablespoonfuls each of cornstarch and sugar. Add one beaten egg and cook in double boiler until thickened. Add a tablespoonful of butter and flavoring to taste.

Cream Sauce à la Hotel Astor.—Beat together one cupful each sugar and butter until perfectly blended. Add cream until mixture is like thick cream, dust with nutmeg or mace and serve.

Delicious Fruit Sauce for Plum Pudding.—Boil together one cupful of water and two of sugar for ten minutes. Thicken slightly with three level teaspoonfuls arrow root or two teaspoonfuls corn starch mixed with a little cold water, simmer five minutes, then add a half cupful candied cherries, cut in halves and a few pistache nuts quartered. Flavor with nutmeg or vanilla as preferred.

Hard Sauce for Plum Pudding.—Beat one cupful of butter to a cream. Add sugar gradually, two cupfuls in all, beating until very light. Add the whites of two eggs beaten to a stiff dry foam. Arrange on a flat glass dish and grate a little nutmeg over it.

Molasses Sauce.—To make molasses sauce, which is an excellent accompaniment to a plain rice or apple pudding, mix together one cupful of molasses, a tablespoonful of vinegar or the juice of one lemon, a saltspoonful of salt and a tablespoonful of butter. Boil ten minutes.

Milton Keynes UK
Ingram Content Group UK Ltd.
UKHW020411240824
447344UK00004B/497

9 789362 094841